Saving Me

Elva Alicia Leon

ACKNOWLEDGMENT

This book couldn't have come to fruition had it not been for the beautiful people who have supported me and continue to support me on this amazing journey called life.

First, I would like to thank my mother who encouraged me to share our story of struggle so that others may find hope and peace. Thank you for finding the strength to choose loving us over your addiction. *Te Quiero Mucho.*

To Myra: Thank you for sacrificing so much for me. I am the person I am today because you not only cared for me but you believed in me and for that I am truly grateful. I love you immensely.

To Veronica: Thank you for being there for Jessica and me. I can't thank you enough for helping me during my college years. I love you very much.

To my niece and nephews: I love you and I hope my story reminds you that you can do anything you set your heart to.

To Jessica: There are no words to describe the amount of unconditional love that I have for you and that is amazing. My heart lights up when I look at you and the love I feel wants to burst through. Thank you for hanging in there with me, believing in me but more so believing in yourself. It is through you and for you that my life was given real meaning. Out of all the accomplishments I have achieved, none has been greater than having raised you to be a strong, loving and independent young lady. I am very proud of you.

To my students: When I decided to become a teacher, I thought I would not only teach you academics but I would also teach you about life. I was eager to instill in you the belief that you could do and be anything you wanted to be. I wanted you to leave my classroom, not only more knowledgeable in math and reading, but more importantly, I wanted you to leave being a more compassionate, loving and self-confident person. Little did I know that the greatest lessons that I would be learning about life would come from you.

You shared your own stories of struggle and in so doing I learned to be more compassionate. You helped each other out and that reminded me to be more loving. Most of all, you listened to my story, and at forty years old, encouraged me to fulfill my own dream of writing this book. You believed in me as much as I believed in you. Thank you for asking me about my book every day at school; each time you did it motivated me to keep going, especially on those tough days when I wanted to quit. I am honored to have been your teacher.

To my editor, Peter I. Galace: Thank you very much for turning my story into a beautiful masterpiece. You saw my vision and helped me achieve my dream.

To all of you reading my book: There is a quote that reads, "I don't write for a million people to like me; I write for a million people like me." Please know that although we haven't personally met, I have written this book for you. I have overcome my own fears to expose my darkest moments in life, in hopes that through my own story you find some glimmer of light in yours. Remember that there is light at the end of the tunnel, you just have to keep walking.

CONTENTS

Chapter 1

Baby

"Ring ring." It was one o'clock in the morning. I had just entered the point in dreaming where one is fully immersed in deep sleep. The ringing of the phone was a recognizable sound that awoke me without feeling the drowsiness one has in the morning. It was more a fight or flight response to waking up. My eyes were wide open and all of my senses fully aware.

I quickly grabbed the phone and slid the unlock icon to answer. I didn't even check to see if I recognized the number. All I knew was that something must have been wrong. No one ever calls in the middle of the night unless something extraordinary is happening. I held the phone to my ear, not knowing what I would hear, yet preparing myself for the worst. "Mom, the baby doesn't have a heartbeat!" Through wails and cries I had never heard from my daughter before, she was able to tell me that she was in the hospital and had lost her baby at twelve weeks of pregnancy.

Earlier that day I had spoken to her and she had been complaining of stomach pains. I made it clear to her that something might be wrong with her pregnancy and that she should go to the doctor. Since she lived with her father, I didn't know the extent of her illness, and I had no control whether or not she actually went to the doctor. I felt safe enough to allow my daughter to wait for her boyfriend Martin to take her to the doctor. "Make sure Martin takes you to the emergency room as soon as he gets out of work." Those had been my last words to her before I received her call. Martin and my daughter Jessica had been together for five years, since high school. From the moment I met Martin, I knew he would marry my daughter. Or I hoped he would. He was a sweet and caring soul. He was raised in a traditional Mexican home and had been taught good morals and values. He was the only teen I knew who was very respectful in every way. He came to ask permission to date my daughter and would always offer to help us in any way he could.

I figured she would end up going to the emergency room where she would just be given medicine and sent back home. Nothing too serious. She had struggled with her pregnancy from day one. She would complain of being tired and not hungry. She was very emotional; she would cry for no reason. Her eating habits changed as well. She could no longer stomach the taste or smell of chicken when, before this, chicken was practically all we ate. We ate so much chicken that we often joked we would grow feathers. Slowly, her body was beginning to weaken from the inability to keep her food down.

Two weeks earlier, my daughter called me because she had fainted while on a routine visit to her doctor. She had gone in for a check-up and to get pills to help her with the vomiting when she had a small seizure right there in the examination room. She was rushed to the hospital and was given fluids, then checked, and was given the all clear to go home. I remembered that call. She wasn't nearly as distraught, so I knew it wasn't that serious. I had gone to see her, sat down with her, and we talked about her taking better care of herself. She agreed, and I left. I knew Martin would look after her.

This night however was not the same. After she managed to tell me what had happened, I was in shock myself. I had never expected her to lose this baby. Just days beforehand, she had been so excited, buying baby clothes and making me a Best Grandma in the World jar to put my pencils in to keep at school. She had included a small white bib with yellow words that read The World's Best Grandma. After this tragedy, no one would be calling me grandma, no longer was my grandchild growing safely in my daughter's womb. All I could say was, "I am sorry, Jessica, only God knows why this happened. I'll be right there." I hung up the phone and jumped out of bed. I grabbed a pair of shoes, a sweater, car keys, and rushed out the door. The hospital wasn't far from my house so I knew I would be there quickly. On the drive over there, I began to think of what I could possibly say to her to ease her pain. I couldn't think of any. What do you say to someone who has lost her child, even if it wasn't born yet? It was still a baby, her baby.

I reached the hospital and was escorted to her room. I opened the door to see her sitting on the table and the moment she saw me, she stood up and ran to me. She tried to explain what had happened and between her sobs I heard her ask, "Why did this happen to me?" I did not have an answer other than to say, "I am sorry this happened, we don't understand it now, but I am sure we will one day."

As I stood there holding my baby while her heart was breaking at the loss of her own baby I began to think of the day that her life was close to ending as well. I thought about the emotions I would have felt if I had lost my baby too. I thought about how much love she had for her child and how she was able to so freely show it. Twenty years earlier, at the conception and birth of my daughter, it was a different story.

Chapter 2

Hello Moon and Stars

I was born Elva Alicia Leon. My mother named me after herself, Elva, and the Alicia came from my father's suggestion to name me after his sister. It should have been spelled as one word, Elvalicia, but thank goodness, it was divided into two. I am not too fond of the name Elva, but since my mother chose to name me after her, I decided to use it for professional reasons. I use Elva with people I am not close to and Alicia with friends and family. It's all worked out well so far. I was born in Los Angeles on December 3, 1975, a date that has two of my favorite numbers, 3 and 5. I don't know why, but they are.

My mother, Elva, and my father, Benjamin, were both immigrants from México. My mother came to the US like most immigrants, looking for a better life. She traveled all the way from Monclova, Coahuila, a small town in northern Mexico. Her father had been a railroad worker and her mother a traditional housewife taking care of a husband and fourteen children. My mother was somewhere in the middle, one of four girls. She often described herself as a tomboy back in Mexico, a troublemaker too. She told stories of having lice, taking them out of her hair and putting them in the hair of girls whose beautiful long and flowing hair she envied. As sad as that story was, I found it fascinating that my mother was such a troublemaker.

The story I liked most was where she and some friends would wrap dog poo in wrapping paper and leave it on doorsteps. They would knock, run away and hide, and watch from afar as people opened their doors, see the gift on their doorstep, pick it up with a smile and unwrap it. Obviously, the victims were not very happy at the disgusting surprise. She loved that prank, and I loved to hear her tell the tale. I saw where my love of pranks came from, but mine were not as mean. My worst was hiding in the closet waiting for my daughter to walk by and then jumping out and scaring her. Unfortunately, that time didn't turn out as scary as it was dangerous. I popped out of the closet and slammed the door right on her lip. I didn't time my move correctly and she happened to be right at the door when I pushed it and yelled, "Boo." She was thirteen at the time. I spent the night apologizing and putting ice on her lip. She didn't think it was funny and neither did I. I felt awful seeing her with a swollen lip. The next day she stayed home from school recovering and that made me feel guiltier because she hated missing school.

There was also that time I threw a smoke bomb under my sister's car (I was twenty-five, mind you) and having a mind of its own, the bomb rolled under the neighbor's car. The neighbor's car looked like it was on fire with all that smoke coming out. Thankfully, no one came out to see the spectacle I'd created. Blame it on my mother from whom I inherited making practical jokes.

I know little about my father. He returned to Mexico six months after I was born. The only information I have about him comes from my mother and my sister. Both speak of him as being a tall and gentle loving man. They said he was a good father.

The word father and the idea of calling someone father have always been odd to me. I never quite understood the term; it did not make sense.

There were only two occasions I heard from him after he left. I must have been three years old when my mother, after speaking with someone over the phone, handed it to me and asked me to speak with *"Tu Papá."* Who was this person named Father? Why did I have to talk to him? I took the phone and spoke with some stranger to please my mother. Don't ask what the conversation was about because all I remember is that I wanted to get off the phone as quickly as possible and get back to playing. The second time I heard from him was when my aunt came over after she had vacationed in Mexico. She came back with a box full of small dolls. She and my mother were excited to tell me that they were for me and was from this man called *"Tu Papá."* Again, who was this person and why would he send me gifts? I thought about it for a moment, then went on to play with all of them. It was like Christmas Day.

It took a few years, twenty to be exact, for me to go back and relive those moments and understand the mind of a confused three-year old. After that surreal Christmas Day experience, I didn't hear from him again until the age of 36. What I know about him and how he and my mother met came from stories my mom told me.

He and my mother met while working in a factory in Los Angeles assembling metal tubes for faucets. My mother was thirty-five and my father a few years older. By that time, my mother was raising my two older half-sisters: Myra, who was ten years older than me and Veronica, who was nine years older than me. While I struggled with the fact that it was not right that my mother had children from different fathers, I came to understand that it was not something she had planned. As life would have it, that's the way it turned out. I never judged my mother for that.

When Veronica would get upset, she would remind us that we were only half-sisters. Myra would tell us that regardless of who our fathers were, we were sisters nonetheless. She would say, "We came from the same womb." My mother would swing back and forth. Sometimes we were sisters and other times we were just half-sisters. It depended on what mood she was in. If she was mad at us, we were half-sisters. I gravitated to the fact that we were half-sisters, but it did not matter, I loved them both anyway.

In the beginning of my mother and father's relationship, she had made it clear that she did not want any more children. My mother lived in a small apartment with little furniture when they met. She was trying to raise my older sisters. My father had no children and told my mother that he had been tested and had a medical condition that rendered him unable to have children. Therefore, my mother didn't worry about getting pregnant. Surprise… A few months later, my mother was pregnant — with me.

My mother told me that she was very upset when she found out and wanted to terminate the pregnancy; however, my father refused to give her the money and she refused to pay for it herself. Basically, she didn't want me but didn't want to spend the money to have a doctor end my life. It made total sense, in a cold, detached, penny-pinching kind of way. Every time I heard my mother say those words, they would hurt. They seared my heart. How could my own mother not want me?

I believe that's where the feeling of unworthiness, the feeling of being unwanted and unloved came from. Time after time as she would repeat the story, the pain lessened, but it never quite went away. I learned to bury it in the back of my mind and pretend I never heard it. I learned to protect myself that way because I could not stand up to her and tell her how much it hurt.

My mother said my father was happy to see me come into this world. When she said that part, it eased the pain somewhat. At least my father wanted me. So, my conception was not planned, nor was I wanted by my mother. To top it off, I almost killed her during childbirth. What a way to start out my life!

My mother said she remembered being in the hospital after I was born and her IV came out. She began bleeding and feeling like she was drifting. She talked of this beautiful feeling of leaving her physical body and not wanting to return. It would be a feeling I would later come to feel myself. She talked of not wanting to come back because that feeling of love and peace was all she wanted. I loved to hear the confirmation that when we are dying, we feel nothing but love and peace. At the same time, I felt bad that her near death experience had been my fault. Not only did she not want me, I almost took her life in the process of entering this world. This was a story I heard many, many times and still continue to hear from time to time. She survived, of course, and returned home with my dad and a bundle of joy (me).

I was a source of great joy to my dad. The night I came home from the hospital my father took me outside the house and held me up to the night sky and introduced me to the moon and the stars. My mother said he was so proud to show me off. She on the other hand said that she could not understand how this crazy man thought it was perfectly fine to take a newborn out into the cold night without proper clothes. She said I was just in my diaper. And to add crazy to craziness, he held me up in some kind of a strange ritual. I think this is probably why my love for nature is so strong and why I feel such a strong connection with the universe.

I did not understand why my mother would even care. She didn't want me in the first place so why should she be upset at my father's weird ritualistic way of introducing me to the world. My mother told me how my father and my older sister took care of me for the first six months. I think my mother suffered from postpartum depression. Or more like pre-partum as well as postpartum since she really wanted nothing to do with me beforehand, or afterward. She told the story of my father strapping me to the high chair to keep an eye on me while he cooked. My older sister would pitch in, but according to her, she and my father did not really get along. I guess I became the connection that allowed them to work together. Both loved me and wanted the best for me.

Six months after my birth, my father made the bold decision to pack my bags and drop me off at my aunt's house, my mother's only sister living in California. He had had enough of my mother. Her drinking and smoking had become worse and she would take her aggression out on my father. She had begun drinking seven years earlier when Myra's biological father kidnapped her at the age two and took her to Florida where he had a wife and other children. A whole other family that my mother knew nothing about. My sister was snatched from the babysitter's arms while my mom was at work, put into a car, and taken. The babysitter had tried to save my sister and had hung on to the car that was driving away. She was dragged for a few yards, not wanting to let go of the car door handle. Unfortunately, she was not able to rescue my sister, but her bleeding and raw skinned knees showed she had held on for as long as she could as the car drove off with my sister.

My mother's only child had been kidnapped and she had no clue where she had been taken. When I hear this story, my eyes well up with tears. I can't even begin to imagine the thought of how a mother would feel not knowing where her child was, not knowing if her baby was suffering hunger or pain. Here was my mother, in a different country, in it illegally, who didn't speak English, facing a mother's worst nightmare. Her child had been taken and there was no one she could ask for help. The following days and months of sadness and hopelessness led her to numb her pain in the easiest way possible for her. She began to drink. Beer was her drink of choice. The drinking, made her forget the pain, for a while. My sister was missing for four years.

During that time my mother met another man and had my middle sister, Veronica. Even though she was now in a new relationship and had a new child, her drinking didn't stop. In fact, it progressively got worse. Veronica's dad eventually left my mother as well. Once again, my mother found herself alone with the sole responsibility of raising two young daughters. The loneliness made her drink even more.

Four years after the kidnapping of my older sister Myra, my mother's cousin read an ad in the local Spanish newspaper *La Opinión*. The ad had been written for my mother. My sister's stepmother had placed an ad in the newspaper asking for my mother to contact her so that she could return my sister to her. My mother called the number provided by the newspaper and spoke with the stepmother. The stepmother gave her an address where they would meet and plan the details, so that my sister's father would not find out that my mother would be taking her back. According to my sister, the stepmother did not like her and had made her life miserable. My sister related how she suffered abuse at the hands of her stepmother. The most distressing story was when she spoke of having to eat cereal with cockroaches in it because that's how the stepmother wanted it.

My mother wasted no time and found a friend to help her with the expenses to fly to Miami, Florida to pick up my sister. It must have been such a relief to my mother to hear that my sister was relatively fine and to know where she had been this whole time — Miami, Florida. The return occurred, and my mother came home on a bus with her five-year old little daughter, the daughter she had not seen for over four years. This little girl was a stranger to her and my mother was a stranger to this little girl. My sister did not speak any Spanish and my mother spoke very little English; yet my mother managed to tell my sister they would be going to see her father.

Upon arrival at the house, my sister asked about her father and once again, my mother lied to her and said he was on his way. My mother was so loving towards her that my sister, aged six, asked my mother if she could remain with her. During this whole ordeal, my mother sent Veronica to Mexico to be looked after by her grandmother. She felt that she needed to focus all her time and energy on bringing my sister back and needed Veronica to be well taken care. She figured my grandmother would be the best person to take care of my middle sister.

Once my sister was back home, my mother's main mission was to bond with her, so my middle sister would have to wait a few years to return home.

Part of it was that my grandmother would not let my sister go back and for fear my grandmother might suffer a heart attack. My mother left my sister in Mexico longer than planned.

Through all of this, beer had become my mother's best friend. Her drinking was not yet extreme but severe enough to affect their home life and relationship.

When my mother became pregnant with me, my father had issues with her drinking, especially with the fact that she was drinking while pregnant with me. My mother refused to stop drinking and my father did everything in his power to make sure she did not drink, so fights would begin. When I was six months old, her drinking and cigarette smoking ways had run my father's patience out. She would become violent and aggressive when she drank. I completely understood how that would take its toll. My father packed his bags and mine and decided I would be better off living with my aunt in Los Angeles. As for him, he decided to return to Mexico. Not sure what he was thinking leaving me with my aunt instead of taking me with him to Mexico. It hurt for a while to feel that I was easily disposable. Just dump a six-month old anywhere. I will never understand how parents could just leave their children and not see them again. There I was, at six months old, living with my aunt, motherless and fatherless.

A few days after my father left me at my aunt's house, my mother came to pick me up. According to her, she felt sorry for me and decided to get me. My sister had something to do with it too. My sister had bonded with me and wanted me back. What a way for me to start my first six months on earth. These six months were the beginning of what would become an adventure. I would say torture, but I have come to realize that it was all part of my journey, so I chose to call it my adventure. I guess after that, my mother had no choice but to bond with me. After all, she was the only person I had to take care of me, who would feed me or bathe me while my older sister was at school. Who would carry me when I cried, if my sister was not there?

Early recollections of life with my sisters and my mom are few. I oftentimes become frustrated that I don't remember many events from my childhood. I think I can count them with my fingers and toes. I tried for a long time to recall events, but gave up after realizing that I must have forgotten them for a reason. My body and my soul did not need to remember those things. I needed protection I guess. Protection from my own experiences. I figured if I remembered those things, they would only cause me more harm. I decided a long time ago not to open up that can of worms. I figured if the worms wanted to come out, they would.

My first memory was of our house in East Los Angeles. I was about four years old. Our house was the smallest house on the block. It was pushed way to the back of the lot. Driving by, you would not think there would be a house there. It was painted a light green color and had small windows and a white door. That, I can picture. I could be making that up, but that's how I remember it. Thinking about it now, it reminds me of a dollhouse: a house that's perfect on the outside and perfect on the inside. Unfortunately, that was not the reality for us. I wanted it to be the truth, but it was not. I loved that house. It had two bedrooms. My sister Veronica slept in one and Myra in the other. The living room had become a bedroom. My mom and I had a queen size bed and a TV there. Then, there was a small kitchen and our bathroom. When I was older I would drive by to visit it. I would sit and stare for a while, trying to remember as much as I could. My life had begun in a weird way, and this house added to its uniqueness.

On Hubbard and Whittier in East Los Angeles, it lay in not the greatest area. A few blocks down, either north or south, one would get the "Cholo" neighborhoods (Cholo, meaning gang member). East LA had its gangs and plenty of them. Though I never associated with them, I did see them. Usually they made their presence known just by being all tattooed with their gang affiliation name. Their attire of khaki shorts and white T-shirts also gave them away. Not everyone who wore khaki shorts or pants and white T-shirts were cholos, but most were. I knew this because my sister Veronica dressed like a chola, but she was not one. She wore khaki pants, long shirts and she wore the chola makeup, black lipstick and thick black eyeliner with black mascara. She went heavy on the blush too. She even had a chola name — Tiny. They called her Tiny because she was short, petite I like to say. My mom said she was short because she didn't drink enough milk while she was in Mexico. But that was never proven.

Our neighborhood consisted of mostly Mexican families. Some were restaurant workers, housekeepers and factory workers. Honest and hardworking.

Making a living any way they knew how. There were also the wives who stayed at home. My mom knew a few of them. I remember most seemed to live as complete families, meaning there was a mother and a father in the home. I am sure there were single parent homes, but the two-parent homes always caught my attention. I always found their situation strange. We did not have a male figure in our home, so I often wondered how or why other homes had one. It's weird that five-year olds would wonder about such things. One would think that the minds of five-year olds are on toys and games and food. But no, they start to question life as well. At least I did. I remember our neighborhood was filled with children. Some of them would play with me, while others would just pass by, not acknowledging my presence. I knew them from afar, but never their names or their stories.

Across our home lived a family with three young kids. I think they were about my age because I remember playing with them and they were not much taller than me, two boys and one girl. I don't remember their names, but I remember they came from a two-parent home. I think I was a little jealous of that. I recall the kids asking their dad for permission to do things. I never had to ask for permission. I would just get up and go. I somehow ended up in their home on most days. I would eat there sometimes. I don't know if it was because my mom did not prepare food or because I just liked being there. I wasn't malnourished or starving. I didn't want to give the impression that I was in dire need of food.

Come to think of it, this was the time my mother's drinking had become worse, so maybe the family felt sorry for me and fed me. It was nice of them. I also remember spending some Christmas times there, opening gifts with them as though they were my family. I don't think my mom was there, maybe she was. It was great being part of an intact family for the holidays, even if it was not my own. At five, my anticipation was on what gift I would get and that I was surrounded by people with whom I could share the moment.

Chapter 3

Please Help

I can't remember my mother much during my childhood but for the mere glimpses of the tragedies that occurred in our home. While other children can recall times of baking cookies with their mothers and their mothers singing to them, I can't remember my mother doing those things. I know my sister did some of those things with me because I have pictures celebrating my birthday and my older sister being so proud to help me cut the cake. I can't say much about my middle sister. I don't think we bonded much. My older sister was more like my mother. It felt like she was just a caretaker or visitor of some sort. My older sister said that the responsibility of taking care of me fell mostly on her. I felt bad hearing her say those things. I often felt like I was a burden.

At fifteen Myra should have been enjoying her life, doing teenage stuff hanging out with friends and shopping. Instead she had to take care of me, go to school, and work at the same time. I remember her preparing my bottles. I would often become quite demanding with my bottle and how it was prepared. "Warm milk and oatmeal inside!" I would yell at her. She would do it because she loved me and because my mother would yell at her if she didn't. She would also bake me cakes on my birthdays. I remember her bathing me and singing to me as well. All those things that moms should do, my sister did. When I ask Myra to tell me stories of raising me, she speaks of me as if I were her own child. She tells the stories with so much love. Knowing how she struggled to go to work, go to school and take care of me fills my heart with so much gratitude and love. She did this without owning a car. She took the bus everywhere. Needless to say, I saw her as a mother more than I did my own mother.

At Hubbard Street, my mother was drinking every other day. Some days her drinking was heavy and some days were light, a beer or two. On days she drank heavily, she would become extremely angry. I think she would get drunk to unleash her anger towards life. Unfortunately, she would take her anger out on both of my sisters. By this time, my middle sister Veronica had returned and had been living with us for a few years. My mother had taken her to Mexico to be watched by my grandmother while my mother went to pick up my older sister from the evil stepmother. After that ordeal was squared away and once she was settled with my older sister, she was ready to bring Veronica back. Things were not so simple though, my grandma did not want to give her up. My mother said she fought hard to bring Veronica back to the United States. My grandmother suffered a heart attack at the thought of my sister being taken away, so my mother left her in Mexico. When my sister was nine years old, my grandmother passed away and my mother was able to bring her back. While my sister was in Mexico, my mother made sure she sent money every month, so that my grandmother and my sister had everything that they needed.

Nine years of not bonding with Veronica took its toll on my mother. Not surprisingly, the lack of bonding with both daughters made it easier for my mother to beat them. My mother would get drunk and often wake them up by yelling at them. It did not matter to my mother if they had school or work the next day. She did not care what time of the night it was. Her beatings did not have a schedule. She would go into their rooms and demand that they go into the living room where she would insult them by calling them some of the worst names a human being could say to another. Cold and calloused, she would continue by slapping them. The slaps would turn into using her bare hands to punch them in the face. Neither of my sisters would retaliate, they would not put up a fight. As if using her bare hands was not hard enough to watch, I once saw her use an extension cord to "whip them." She would leave gashes and open wounds on their bodies. Seeing bruises on my sisters was normal for me. I was about four when I remember the beatings beginning. I was filled with emotions during that time. I was confused, scared and sad.

Confused as to what they could have possibly done to deserve such gruesome beatings. Confused as to why I was not included in the beatings and scared that I would get beaten too. Mostly, I was sad to see my sisters cry. One thing I knew for sure was that this beer would turn her into a totally different person, an evil person. I hated the sight of those cans.

One particular night, the night I considered a nightmare, began like a dream. All was well until the evening. My mother had been drinking all day, and it was usually only at night when she would be drunk enough and build up enough anger to beat my sisters. In her sadistic and ritualistic way, my mother woke Myra up with her yelling as well and demanded she go to the living room. I woke up to her yelling. Once my sister was in the living room, my mother punched, scratched and pulled my sister's hair without mercy. Blood covered her face and her hair was left a tangled mess. Her clothes were torn and her spirit broken. All I could do was to watch. Watch and wish it would be over soon. I wanted to help her, but didn't know how. I could feel the bubble of sadness in my stomach, the bubble of helplessness built up. Yet there was nothing I could do. I could see something different in my sister's eyes that night. I saw anger in her that I had not seen before. She was fed up and had had enough of the beatings. She did not put up a fight, but was close to it. I could feel my sister's anger welling up and her wanting to beat my mother as well.

My sister called her boyfriend to pick her up after the beating. I think my sister must have been hiding somewhere until her boyfriend picked her up because I did not see her for a while after that. I don't know how my sister got away, but I was sure glad she did, otherwise my mom would have killed her. All of my mom's anger was focused on my Myra because Veronica had stayed over at our aunt's house. I clearly remember Myra running out of the front door and into her boyfriend's car. I remember my mother screaming and running after her while I was running after both of them. My sister hopped into the car that was parked in the middle of the street, her boyfriend just waiting for her to close the door so he could speed off. My sister managed to race into the car and close the door immediately. But she did not lock it and my mother, who was just a few steps away, managed to open the door and hang onto it with both hands. What happened next was surreal, something one would only see in the movies. My sister's boyfriend took off with my mother hanging onto the door. My mother's goal was to pull my sister out of the car and continue to beat her. My sister's boyfriend's goal was to save her. I was rooting for him. I wanted my sister saved. The commotion on the street was immense. My sister, yelling for my mother to let go, and my mother yelling as she was being dragged across the street.

At the top of this four-year old's lungs, I was screaming for help. My mother was dragged a few feet until she could no longer hold on. I saw her fall onto the hard and dark pavement, face down. It took her a few moments to regain her strength then she stood up. Her knees were bloody from being scraped across the rough pavement, and I could see pieces of raw skin hanging off when she stood up. Once she stood up, I stopped yelling. I stopped for two reasons: one, my mother had let go and my sister had been saved; two, nobody came out to help anyway. To this day, I don't know how not one person came out to help. I can't understand how an entire neighborhood could ignore the painful screams for help of a four-year old. I stood in the middle of this dimly lit and lonely street and watched my mother standing there, bleeding from her knees.

That night confirmed my suspicions that nobody cared about me except my sister Myra, and she was gone. I was alone in this world. This lesson would haunt me forever. I don't know what happened after that because my memory, my nightmare, led me to what happened the next morning. My sister could no longer take the abuse at home, so at fifteen, she had no choice but to leave the house. It was a life or death decision-making situation. At that time, being only four, I was angry at her. The only person I had bonded with, the mother figure who I felt safe with was leaving me.

I remember her coming home the next day to pack her belongings. She knew it would be safe to come home because my mom never drank two days in a row. The day after she drank, she would be dealing with her hangover and her regrets. My mom, now sober and not knowing exactly what had happened the night before, except it was not good at the sight of my sister's injuries, begged my sister for forgiveness. She did that often — beg for forgiveness. She pleaded with my sister to stay. After seeing my sister's bruises and open gashes, she felt remorse. My sister knew better. So many times she had apologized only to go back on her word and hurt her again. My sister had to leave. I was devastated. She placed all her stuff in boxes and as she was doing that, I would take them out when she was not looking. In the mind of this four-year old, I thought I had planned it perfectly. I would take her stuff out of the boxes and put them back in their place. Her makeup back in her dresser drawers, her clothes back in the closet, neatly hung and her shoes exactly where they had always been. I did not want her to go, and I was going to stop her from leaving.

At such a young age, I did not have the words to express how much I needed her. I felt the pain and hurt and sadness, but I couldn't say it. My little hands could not unpack fast enough. I was too slow and afraid she would see me. Except for the few things I had taken out of the boxes, she managed to get them all and leave.

My soul was shattered and my heart was broken into a million pieces. I felt helpless. I felt hopeless. All I could do was keep some of her things, things that would remind me of her. I wanted to know and feel that she was with me even though she was not. And maybe, just maybe, she would realize her stuff was missing and she would come back to get it and get me, too. I did not remember seeing her leave. I guess I did not want to because I did not want the pain of seeing her leave me. Thank goodness our brain blocks out some things which we have no wish to return to.

Chapter 4

Treasures

I often sit and look at our old pictures and remember the good times in that old green house. I remember my older sister putting makeup on me. And then there was the time when I was playing with matches in Veronica's room when I was called in to take a bath, I quickly blew them out. At least I thought I had. A few minutes after I had jumped in for my bath, all three of them came running, yelling and screaming into the bathroom and began taking water out of my tub. One bucket after another, they would run in and out just like a very well set up system. The matches I had played with had not completely extinguished, and Vero's mattress had caught fire. I did not know what all the commotion was about. The words they were shouting came too fast and loud for me to understand. Thankfully the fire was put out and nobody other than the mattress was destroyed. My mother decided to have a chat with me and showed me the burnt mattress. Needless to say, I was not allowed to play with matches after that.

It was in this house that I made my first major decision. At the age of almost five I decided to no longer drink out of a baby bottle. Actually, I was kind of forced to make the decision. My house had no rules and my mother allowed me to drink out of a bottle any time I wanted. I would often ask my older sister to fix me my bottles. She would complain and say I was five years old and it was time I was off the bottle. She would prepare it for me anyway. Now that she was gone, my bottle drinking days were not as frequent. My bottle addiction came to an abrupt end one day.

After school my best friend came to visit and caught me drinking out of a bottle. I was lying in bed, watching cartoons and drinking my baby bottle with warm strawberry milk when suddenly my best friend walked through the door and saw me. I was not expecting anyone because we had just come back from kindergarten. The embarrassment is still fresh in my mind. Five-year olds can experience embarrassment, and boy, did I feel it that day! I quickly removed the bottle from my mouth, hid it under the pillow (even though it was too late, she had already seen me) and pretended nothing had happened. That day I swore I would never ever drink out of a bottle again.

My kindergarten year was the year I learned what real love was. I fell in love with an old doll that my mother and I found in a trash can. When my mother and I went to the liquor store, we would walk through an alley. It did not take us long to get to the store because it was not very far. I enjoyed going there because an Asian couple owned it, and I always found it fascinating to hear them speak Spanish. They knew us and would often strike up a conversation. We would take trips not so much for groceries but because my mom needed her beer.

On one of our walks through the alley, my mother decided to look through someone's trash. She would often find things of value and take them home. That day she found something that became very valuable to me — a doll. This was no ordinary doll. I had never seen one like her. She was the size of a newborn. Her face was sweet and loving. She had dark eyes and her dark hair was made from the same soft plastic as the rest of her body. What stood out to me was her skin. It was a beautiful dark mocha color and really soft. She felt so real. I named her "Carnita," Spanish for meat. I remember my mother saying that she felt as if she was made of real flesh. She was like a real baby.

Looking back on that day, taking her out of the trash can was meant to happen. It was like she was waiting for me. I could tell she had been a bit neglected. Her soft brown skin had been scribbled all over with a pen, but my mother was able to clean that off. She also had a few places where some plastic was missing. Nonetheless, I loved that doll like no other. Before that, I didn't really like dolls much. But Carnita was special. The saying "Someone's trash is someone else's treasure" is so true. She was my treasure. You might be thinking that we must have been super poor for my mother not to be able to afford to buy me a doll. The truth is that we weren't. We were not rich, but we were not extremely poor either. My mother worked and also received government assistance, so she always had enough to provide for us. The problem was (according to my older sister) she did not really care to shop for food or furniture. Her drinking might have had something to do with that.

Myra makes me laugh so hard when she tells the story of her slapping my middle sister in the face over the last egg and sausage. She says she was hungry and when she went to look in the refrigerator, the only things inside were one egg and one sausage. Myra set out the food on the counter so that she could make herself a meal but then had to go use the bathroom. Veronica came out of her room at that moment and saw the food on the counter. She decided to cook it for herself. Before she could eat it, Myra came out and a fight began. Myra slapped Veronica for having the audacity to cook herself a meal with the food she had set out. Needless to say, Myra reclaimed her meal.

Poor money management led to some hungry nights for my sisters and perhaps for me, too, but I don't remember. As for the doll, I don't know what happened to her. All I know is that she really meant a lot to me. I loved her very much. I often stroll through the toy section and am reminded of her when I see those bright shiny dolls waiting to be adopted off the shelves. The thought of her being at the bottom of some heap of garbage makes me sad. One might think that I saved her from the trash, from being dumped at the bottom of some garbage dump. The truth is that she saved me from many lonely nights when my sisters were gone and my mother had passed out cold from drinking.

I was five years old when we moved to El Monte where my mother had been working as a housekeeper for a family. She would wash their dishes, clean their house, do their laundry and even mow their lawn. My mother was a jack of all trades. This was a time when I don't recall being too close with my mom, but I admired her hard work. She would feed me and we would take the bus together to wherever her next housekeeping job would be. I don't think we ever had conversations on those journeys. I remember taking the bus, but always being quiet. Next door to the house my mother cleaned lived a man by himself. He must have been impressed with my mother's work ethic because my mother could clean like no other. She was a tornado of cleanliness.

I could see how my stepfather fell in love with her. My mother was a woman raising a small child on her own, cleaning houses for a living and not stopping at just cleaning, but mowing the lawns too. It may be relevant to mention that she was beautiful. Aside from her smoking and drinking habits, which I don't think he knew about, she was something else. She was also funny — she was funny when she was not drinking.

At this stage, my memories are a little clearer. Not by a lot, but enough to write my stories thank goodness. So, my stepfather and mother fell in love. We moved into his house and we all thought things would be different. I did not know the concept of a family, but I was happy that I had a male figure in the house. Both my sisters came back to live with us. The oldest had been living with her boyfriend and the middle one with an aunt. Little did we know that my mother's drinking would get worse, especially because my stepfather also enjoyed drinking. Only now, she had more people to take her anger out on and since she did not have to work anymore, she had more time to drink. And did she ever.

Chapter 5

Why Not Me

During my mother's drinking sprees, I was the one she would spare. She would take her wrath out on my sisters, but for some reason, never on me. However, I saw it all. That took a toll on me possibly more so than if I had been hit myself. I continued to watch my mother wake my sisters up during the night to beat them with her bare hands for no apparent reason. The beatings would increase in intensity. She would slap and punch them harder each time. There were many instances when she would drag them across the room and out into the middle of the street by their hair. The screaming and pleading for help brought no one to help them. My stepfather would never get involved. Oftentimes, he would leave early in the day knowing how terrible things would become at night. My mother would start drinking once we all left for school, or in my older sister's case, to work. Because she had to constantly leave home to live with friends, she had no choice but to drop out of college and get a job.

I recall becoming aware of my mother's drinking routine. She would drink one day, have a hangover the next, rest, and drink again the next day. That routine went on for years. We all knew it very well. We also smelled it in the air. For some reason we could all smell the beer in the air on the days she would drink. I learned of this after my sisters and I had a conversation regarding her drinking. We found it odd how all of us could smell the acidic, tart odor of beer. It was as if the universe was warning us of impending danger. There was something different in the air that would notify us that it was going to be a "bad day." My suspicions would be confirmed as soon as I got off the school bus. If she wasn't at the bus stop for me or anywhere near it, it was because she was drinking. Another clue that confirmed she was drinking was if the house was spotlessly clean. The only time my mother would clean the house until it was immaculate, I mean shiny, impeccable clean, was when beer was involved. She would hide them under the sink and pretend nothing was going on. We knew better. She would be extremely attentive and very nice as well. This lasted for a few hours or until one of my sisters or my stepfather would come home. Then all hell would break loose.

I tried to think of the worst fight I'd ever seen between my sisters and my mother or my mother and stepfather and they all come up as equally horrific. Those moments were the times where I learned what hopelessness felt like. This was the time where death was so close I could smell it. I was between six and seven when things really got out of hand. Fights and the police in my home were a constant.

Thinking back on those memories makes me realize that even though I was in the midst of terrible living circumstances, I never felt alone. It was like someone was around me; I can't explain it, I just knew. I could not tell you whose presence was there, but in our house, I never felt alone. I know now that they were angels and that they were there to look after us. That is why death never touched our home. At least I truly believed that.

The fighting began with my mother yelling and cursing at my sisters. The curse words would be in Spanish; somehow Spanish curse words sounded more horrible than English curse words. If only one sister was there, she would get my mother's full wrath. The yelling and cursing would quickly turn violent. One evening, Veronica, who was sixteen at the time, came home shortly after eleven at night. She had taken several buses to make it home from Down-town Los Angeles where she worked at a shoe store. It must have taken her over two hours to get home. That day was a "bad day." My mother had been drinking all day and she and my stepfather had gotten into an argument. He was smart enough to leave before dark and before things got worse. The only two people there were my mother and me, and she never laid a hand on me.

The moment my sister came home, my mother rushed to the door to meet her and began cursing at her. My sister had just placed her bus pass and some money on the counter by the door and had taken but two steps inside the house when my mother ran toward her from the kitchen and grabbed her by the neck and threw her down on the floor. Everything happened so quickly, it felt like microseconds. My mother then straddled my sister and began punching, scratching and ripping her clothes. I was standing in the living room, just a few feet away from them, scared to death. The evil look on my mother's face, the scared look in my sister's eyes are memories I will never forget.

One thought ran through my mind — it was my sister's time to die. The look on her face made me believe that. I was sure of it. At one point, my mother had her hands tightly gripped around my sister's neck and my sister was gasping for breath. My sister was a petite little thing, not much taller than 4 feet 11 inches. Thin framed, she could not have weighed more than 110 pounds. My gut feeling told me she had no chance against my mother who was of a thicker built, stronger and taller. Her face was turning purple. Both of my sister's hands grabbed my mother's in a desperate attempt to free herself from being choked. Unable to get herself up or move much, there she lay struggling. I did not know what to do or how to help. I had already learned that yelling for help would not do anything, so I did the only thing I knew to do, I ran as fast as I could and hid in my bedroom closet.

It was a small closet that I would sometimes share with my sisters. I did not have many clothes and neither did they, since they were always coming and going. Lately, they had not been staying there much. They would stay only on "good days" — when my mom would not drink. At age seven I could sit and stretch my legs and still have ample space to move around. It was a dark, peaceful and safe place. The hanging clothes kept me snug and the walls kept me safe. I would hide in there and pretend I was in some imaginary world.

The darkness of the closet allowed me to fill my mind with beautiful colors, sights and sounds. I would drown out all sounds of gasping and yelling, sounds of crying and pleading for help, sounds of glass and dishes breaking. Those sounds would be replaced with a running creek in some beautiful forest. In my imaginary forest, all the trees were green and lush and all the animals lived in harmony. There were no people in my imaginary world, only animals. I saw playful monkeys and strong and loving lions, zebras and even unicorns. They all existed in my world. I would go into the closet and explore the forest with my animal friends until the fighting between my mother and stepfather would end. It usually would last a few hours. I would fall asleep while imagining I was somewhere else. I learned to fall asleep even when the yelling was going on and then when the police came to stop it and ask my stepfather to leave, I would wake up. The silence would wake me up.

This night, however, I could not sleep. I was listening to my sister scream in between trying to gasp for breath. I had my ear to the wall and I could hear her muffled cries. She was begging for someone to help her. Nobody else was there and I could not help her. I did not know how. So, there I was in the closet, trying to figure out what I could do to save my sister.

All of a sudden, I remembered that I had once heard someone talk about prayer. I learned at the church next door that if you prayed to someone named "God" he would magically help. This God lived above the blue sky in a place called Heaven. "Church people" sang to him and asked him for help. They would hold their hands up and look up toward the ceiling. I saw this when I would go over to play with the kids who lived in the church next door to us. They said that all we had to do was talk to him and he would hear us. That much I understood when going over to the church next door.

That night, in the closet, I did something different, something I had never done before. I prayed. I prayed to God. I raised my hands just like the people at church and looked up at the dark ceiling in the closet. I was hoping he knew who I was. I had never spoken to him before; never really introduced myself. In my home, God had been someone my mother would mention briefly, but never took the time to fully explain. He was someone that I did not know about because the only times we went to church were for special events like a baptism, or when the church people asked me to go over and participate in the children's classes. Apparently my school did not know about him either because they never talked about him. I say "He" because to me God sounded like it was a man. That night something in my gut, in the deepest part of my small soul prompted me to ask this "Being" for help. "God, if you can hear me, could you please help my sister?" My eyes closed and my mind focused on getting my message to him. During the entire time, I had my ear to the wall listening to the commotion when suddenly all went silent. My heart stopped and my blood rose with a surge of heat. "She's dead," My sister was dead. I must have been late in asking for help or maybe I should have asked in a louder voice, was what I thought.

I slowly opened the closet door and tiptoed my way to the living room. I needed to see why everything had gone quiet. I was expecting to see the worst. I was expecting to see my sister's lifeless body on the floor, bloodied and beaten. I expected to see gashes with blood flowing from them as I had seen them before. I was expecting to see my mother sitting next to her, crying and filled with remorse at what she had done. After years of brutality I knew my mother would one day go that far. This was something a child should never have to see. But that was not the case. To my surprise, my prayer had worked. I had prayed to this God person and he had helped my sister. She had escaped. As I entered the living room, all the lights were on, but there was no sign of my sister or my mother. The first thing that caught my eye was my sister's bus pass and money still on the counter. My first thought was that she could not have left without them. I grabbed her bus pass and money and quietly walked out to the front yard. I had to give them to her so that she could leave. Without money her chances of going anywhere were slim, and staying was not an option.

I could hear my mother screaming outside. She was not done with her yet. My mind raced, "Please don't find her." I walked in the opposite direction of where my mother was, so when she was in the front yard, I went around the back of the house. In the dark of night, I softly whispered her name, "Vero, are you here?" No answer. I knew better than to speak loudly. I was not about to give my mother any clues as to where she was. I kept walking until I reached the far end of the back yard. I called out to her again. She whispered back. "I'm here, behind the doghouse." I ran to her and saw her in a disheveled state. Her clothes all torn and her face bloodied, her hair tangled, a sight too familiar to me.

Even though I had seen this many times, it tore my heart to pieces each time I saw either sister scratched or bloodied with swollen faces. I wished I could have warned her somehow, spared her from cruel beatings. All I could do to feel like I had some part in saving her was to give her belongings and stand guard for her. As I handed her the bus pass and the few dollars she had come with, she began to sob. My heart was broken. At midnight, bloodied and battered, my sister took the bus back downtown to stay at our aunt's house.

Relief set in. May heart ached with sadness. It should have been me my mother beat. My sisters had had enough. "It should have been me," was all I thought as I watched her escape. I went back inside the house and found my mother passed out on the sofa with all the lights on and mariachi music playing loudly. I grabbed a blanket and a pillow and I lay down on the floor next to her. I was an expert at drowning out sounds, so the music and the lights would not be a problem. I was really tired, too, so I covered myself up and thought about the night's event. I had prayed to "God" to save my sister, and he did. This "God" was real. I decided I would do more praying. I closed my eyes and fell asleep. I had school the next day.

Chapter 6

My Safe Haven

School was my safe haven, my protective tree house. It was a place I would go to get away from all that was happening at home. Math and reading would allow me to forget the sadness and dysfunction of a place that should have been loving and safe. School was my second home. I looked forward to going even though I was an outcast when I was there. As far as I can remember, I have always been awkward. I did not have many friends mainly because all the kids at school knew about my situation. They knew that my mom was a "drunk." They knew that in my home there were fights, violent fights. The cops were there every other day. One kid would tell another, and another would tell another and before you know it, the whole school knew. They all knew that my mother would drink and pick fights with anyone passing by our street. They knew she would fight with my stepdad and would beat my sisters. They would see her wobble out, drunk, only to get herself more beer.

My behavior also gave our home situation away. I was a loner and did not know how to make friends. I was scared of what people would ask if I started talking to them. What would I say about my clothes not matching on certain days? How would I explain the bags under my eyes from not sleeping? My unkempt, tangled hair? Most of all, what would I say if they asked me about my mother? I did not need any of that. I stayed away from most kids. At times, if it was safe, I would blend in as quietly as I could. At school I was known as the "dumb" student. My classmates labeled me that because I had a tutor.

I had difficulty reading, and math was a huge challenge. I would sit with a tutor at the kidney table in the back of the class for extra help on a daily basis. I had mixed emotions about it. Part of me felt embarrassed about sitting in the back by myself to learn to read, especially because I missed out on what the rest of the class had done and also because other kids would pick on me. Even so, another part of me was grateful as I understood I had trouble learning. I was grateful that someone cared enough to help me learn.

The thing that haunts me the most about school is the question of how the teachers or the office workers, the cafeteria workers or noon supervisors did not notice that something was wrong. Did the teachers not notice the bags under my eyes? Did they not wonder why I never did homework or why I was so quiet? Or they just did not care. Had they asked I would have told them, "My mom is a drunk so school is not a priority" (in an eight-year old's way). But they never asked, and I never shared. Besides, my thoughts were, "How could they understand even if I did tell?" My other thought was, "If no one at home or in my neighborhood cares, why would they?" A huge part of me felt the teachers knew my situation but they did not want to get involved. I think they never asked me for my homework because they knew. While they were strict in demanding homework from other students, I was left alone. Honestly, I don't know how I could have survived if I had to deal with teachers being mean or rude for not bringing homework. Instead, they allowed me to skip homework and they treated me differently, a nice kind of different. I think that's why school felt safe. In a weird way, I felt loved there.

During class, I would be the teacher's helper. I would pass out papers and sharpen pencils. Simple jobs they asked me to do made me feel important. I felt like I could help in some way. At home I could not help my sisters when they were being beaten, or my mother, or my stepfather. I could not help anyone. That sense of helplessness ate me up. It made me feel worthless. At school, it was different. It was like my soul, that little light inside me, could come out. It would come out in the classroom with my teachers. I was someone, someone who mattered.

Growing up and being told that I had been a mistake was forgotten. Maybe I really was not a mistake. My teachers needed me. They needed me to pass out papers and sharpen pencils, and I did my jobs to the best of my ability.

Recess and lunch, however, were different. I dreaded walking out to have "fun" because it was not fun. I never knew if I would have anyone to play with. Most of the time, no one wanted to play with me unless it was a new student who did not know about my life. Sometimes I would forget, and I would feel somewhat normal. Normal enough to join in and play tetherball or handball. Most days, however, I would wander aimlessly around school watching others play. Even my own next-door neighbors, Natalie, who was in second grade when I was in third and Rebecca, a sixth grader, wouldn't play with me. They were the daughters of the lady whose house my mother cleaned. They came from a two-parent, and what seemed to me to be "normal" homes. They did things as a family, and I never saw fighting. My mother stopped being their housekeeper once we moved in with my stepfather. I would go over to their house once in a while to play, but at school, it was different. I felt like they did not want to be seen playing with me. They were embarrassed to be seen with a girl who came from a dysfunctional home. It broke my heart, but I understood. Natalie and Rebecca, however, did look after me from afar. If I had a bully or someone was talking about me or my home life, they would confront that kid. Although everyone knew about my living conditions, it was not to be spoken about.

Going back to the homework situation, there was one time I attempted to complete a homework. I was given an assignment to make a family tree. I was excited to go home, complete it, and return it the next day. I left school with the paper in my hand and boarded the school bus. As soon as I approached the bus, I could already smell it, that disgusting odor of beer. The feeling of sadness quickly overcame me. The overcast and dreary sky added to the churning stomach pain of fear that I felt when I knew it would be a bad day. When I got off the bus, my mother was not waiting for me. My suspicions were validated. When she drank, she would forget to pick me up. That was actually fine with me since having our neighbors and my friends see her drunk embarrassed me. The bus parked across the street from our house so I did not have to walk much. I knew to look both ways before crossing a wide and busy street. I got off the bus, homework and all, and passed all the other parents waiting for their children — moms and dads eagerly anticipating hugging their kids after a long day at school. I crossed the street and as soon as I opened the gate, my mind prepared for a "bad day."

The front door was wide open and so was the screen door. When my mother drank, she did not care about closing anything. Windows and doors were opened all the way. As soon as I entered the house, I saw that it was spotless clean. Bleach and all. I did not see her at first, but then she came inside through the back door. I don't know what happened after that, except that a few hours later she and my stepfather began to fight. Dishes were thrown everywhere and pots and pans were flying across our living room and kitchen, missing their target (my stepfather) most of the time. I also learned how to dodge those things really well. This day, however, things were so bad I had to call my sister. Things had escalated to a full on beating and I could not handle watching my mother getting punched and thrown across the room by my stepfather. My older sister was living in Los Angeles with her boyfriend, and I begged her to pick me up. I packed a few belongings and waited in the closet for a while. Just when I knew it had been long enough, I ran out the front door. I desperately searched for her, waiting for her to come get me. She picked me up, and cried on the car ride to her apartment.

She lived in a complex that had a swimming pool in the center courtyard — the most beautiful pool I'd ever seen. That was my first time visiting her there. She had lived with her boyfriend's family before that, so I was not able to visit much. As we entered her apartment, the phone rang. My sister answered, and it was my mother. My mother had tried to look for me and realized that I was gone. She had known to call her first. She was screaming over the phone and cursing at her. I could hear bits and pieces of her screaming as I stood next to my sister. My sister told my mom that I would be staying with her that night and not to call anymore. She hung up, but my mother was not going to give up. She kept calling and calling. The phone rang incessantly. My sister picked up the receiver, placed a towel around it and set it down. "Don't answer the phone or talk to Mom whatever you do," she said. She triple-covered it with another towel and a pillow because, somehow, my mother's voice could still be heard. She went on to tell me that she would be leaving to run errands for a few hours, to lock the door and not go outside. I was upset. I had called my sister because I was scared and felt alone and I thought she would comfort me, and we would watch TV together. Instead, she was leaving me.

A few minutes after she left, I began to feel anxious and scared. It was dark, and not a soul could be seen around the complex. There I was, alone, with my mother on the phone. As much as I wanted to speak with my mom, I was scared of what she would say. I pushed the door wide open and sat on the floor near the doorway, staring intently at the pool as the sun began to set. Staring at the pool creeped me out even more, so I returned inside, shut the door, and picked up the phone.

"Alicia, Alicia, are you there?" my mother asked. "Yes, mom, I'm here," I responded. "Tell Myra that I am going to call the police and tell them to go arrest her boyfriend because he sells drugs," she screamed. "Oh my God! My sister's boyfriend sells drugs?" I could not believe what I had just heard. My mother could be a lot of things, but she was not a liar. I regretted answering the phone. I quickly hung up and thought for a moment. I knew my mother would follow through on her threat.

I had to do something fast. What if there were drugs in the house like my mom said? What if the police came and arrested her? That was the last thing I needed. The last thing she needed. I remembered that she had a friend she spoke about who lived in the same apartment complex. "My friend's name is Judy," she said. "If you need anything, she lives right across in apartment 112. If you need something or have an emergency, go knock on her door." This was an emergency. I ran past the pool to the other side of the complex, straight to her door. I knocked hard until my fists were bright red and were throbbing with pain. It did not take long for the door to open and a pretty young girl was standing there staring at me. She was almost as pretty as my sister. I told her what was happening. She was the only one who could possibly get hold of my sister. I explained to her who I was and what my mother had said. All I wanted her to do was to call my sister, but instead she yelled to her boyfriend and they mumbled something. Next thing I knew, they were running in and out of my sister's boyfriend's house carrying brown boxes. "Oh no," I thought. My mother was right. I did not know exactly what was in those boxes, but I knew it was not good if they needed to be taken out before the police came. They had been able to call my sister, and she came home quickly. The police never showed up, but we were all shaken up.

We stayed up a little late and after the exhaustion set in, she sent me to bed on the sofa in her living room. There was still one problem though, I was still scared and lonely and confused. But how could I tell her? I did not know how. I tried to go to sleep, but my fear kept me awake. Another night without sleep — it was of course what I had been used to. The next morning, and without incident, she dropped me off at school, of course without my homework. I was the only one that day who did not present her family tree to the class. Once again the teacher did not ask me why I had not completed it. That was life at Monte Vista Elementary until third grade.

Chapter 7

Animals Are Angels Too

S chool was my getaway during the day, and when I was home, my animals were my companions. I have pleasant memories of those times. That's where my love of and bond with animals grew. Since I had no one to talk to or play with, I turned to my animals. At that time, my neighborhood was horse property. That meant we could own any kind of animal we wanted and since we had a humongous backyard, we did. We had pigs, chickens, cows, rabbits, birds, cats and dogs. Even though it was horse property and we could technically own horses, those were the only animals we did not have.

My bond with animals went beyond just pet and owner, they were my friends and protectors, even the pigs. My stepfather bought the pigs to make money from them. He would raise them and feed them well until it was time for them to be shot and butchered for meat. Raising the animals and selling the meat was not only an extra source of income for my stepfather but also a hobby. He was actually a full time construction worker for a huge company that literally built the city of El Monte from the ground up. He laid cement for many of the streets in our city. Although the animals were my friends, I knew better than to bond too closely with them. The pain of losing them when they got killed would be unbearable.

I was five when I had my first experience bonding with a pig, only to later watch it get shot in the forehead, bleed profusely, and die. It was too devastating for me even though it had not been the first time I had an experience witnessing the death of an animal. This was my second experience with the death of an animal but it still took its toll. I was five. Back in that old greenhouse we had a duck. I loved that duck. My mom would feed it every day so it was nice and plump. One day after I came home from school, I noticed that our duck was nowhere in sight. I searched and searched and asked my mother where our duck was. She said she had killed it and had made tamales. The fact that she said it without any emotion or remorse was evil to me. She had grown up in Mexico and that was a normal thing to do, but for me it was not. I protested the tamales and didn't dare touch it when served for dinner. It took a while to heal from the loss of my duck.

We raised some pigs and I loved taking care of them. I would be there during their birth and play with them while they were young piglets. I would often sit and watch the piglets roam around, never straying too far from their mother. I would watch them suckle from their mother when they were hungry, each one fighting for space. The runt is usually the one left without any food. I always felt sorry for it. At times I would pick the chubbiest piglet and detach him from sucking milk and put the runt there instead. Someone had to intervene and I knew I could help. This gave me such a sense of joy. Once I noticed they were getting to about the size when they would be butchered I would distance myself from them. To this day I can see a pig and picture a hole on its brow from a shot to the forehead. It's disturbing.

My chickens were a whole different story. The mother hens were very protective of their young. They would take care of them and made sure that their baby chicks ate before they did. The chicks, all of them, would fit snugly and warmly under their feathers. Watching them, I saw how happy they were. Once in a while, a chick would rear its little head out from underneath all of its mother's belly feathers to see what was going on outside. It would decide that it was too cold and dark and it would hide right back under its mother.

Chickens are funny creatures. Not very affectionate. More of loners I would say, so I could not mingle with them much. They were in their own world on their own mission and bonding with me wasn't it. I loved to sit and watch them. I would make sure they were safe. I was in the chicken coop one day watching the baby chicks hatch from their eggs when I decided that they needed help. The baby chicks would peck slowly at the egg from the inside trying to get out. Watching them struggle made me feel sad for them. "These poor baby chicks must be exhausted from pecking for hours trying to get out," I thought. So I came up with a plan. I would make life easier for them. As they were pecking I too began to slowly peel away the eggshells. I wanted to help. My little fingers would struggle, trying to peel the pieces away. It was a little difficult because the eggshell was stuck to the inside layer that covered the baby chick. I was on a mission, however, to help.

I did not realize that doing that was not helping them at all. I was in fact killing them with each peel. No one explained to me that chicks need to peck away the shell themselves because they know when they are ready to come out. It's amazing how nature hard-wires baby chicks for struggle. I think nature hard-wires all babies for struggle. The chicks already knew to peck slowly, and this allowed their skin to dry and thus prepared them for the climate awaiting them. Rapid eggshell peeling helped compress and wring out their skin because it had not fully dried. Nature knew what it was doing in this area, but I did not. I just peeled away, happy to meet and greet each little wet baby chick. I must have peeled at least four eggs before I became tired and went inside the house. The next morning, I heard it from my mom. It was a "good day," and she sat me down in the kitchen and asked if I had removed the shells of the baby chicks, to which I proudly and quickly responded, "YES!" She very nicely broke the news that all four baby chicks had died. She explained the reason why and I was upset. I had killed four innocent baby chicks with my own hands.

At age nine I had become a murderer. I became like my mother; she had murdered the ducks years back and now I had murdered baby chicks. The only difference was that I had not done it for food. And unlike my mother, I did not grab and twist their necks until the head detached from their bodies, the way she had done to the duck and countless chickens. Nor did I place a gun to their foreheads like my stepfather would do with the pigs, so that they could bleed and die slowly. They were then cut into pieces to sell or make into carnitas (fried pork meat). Yet, I was still a murderer. I had trouble sleeping that night. The guilt ate me up.

The greatest companions I had were my dogs. At one point, we had a dog that had given birth to nine puppies. One night, I took all nine puppies, about four months old, into my bedroom to sleep with me. It happened on one of those "bad days." My mother and stepfather, after a day of drinking, began to argue. As usual, the argument escalated into a full-blown fist fight. I could hear my mother cursing at my stepfather in Spanish and my stepfather cursing back. I came out of my room and ran into the kitchen. I figured that if they saw me, they would stop. It had never worked before, but I always tried. I made it just in time to see my mother pick up a pan she had heated up with cooking oil and twist her arm in an attempt to throw it at my stepfather. My stepfather reacted quickly, grabbed her arm that was holding the pan and turned it around on her. Hot and thick cooking oil splattered onto her face. She screamed a few times, but it did not seem like it really hurt her. My mother's face was burned in blotches. How she did not burn all of her face remains a mystery to me because the pan was full of oil. When the oil reached her skin, it left light red blotches, but slowly they began to worsen and darken to a more blood-like red with some purple mixed in. I stared for a brief moment in disbelief until I could no longer bear to look at her face.

At that point I ran into my "other world," my bedroom closet. I ran inside, closed my eyes and imagined myself back in my magical realm. Every noise was taken over by a quiet breeze in the forest and a clear, running stream. All of my magical animals would return, and I would play with them. I stayed in the closet for a while and as soon as I heard that the kitchen had gone quiet, I walked out. It was over. I often worried if my mom or stepdad would still be alive. I worried a lot for my family. I never knew who would live to see the next day. I knew I would because my mother never hurt me, but there were many times when I was tired and wished that I would go to sleep and not wake up. Many times I wanted it to be me who would not make it to see the next day.

As I walked around, I did not see anyone. The only thing left was the smell of cooking oil and burned skin lingering in the air. I looked for my mother. In the search I spotted my stepfather sleeping outside in the backyard, near the pigs. He would often sleep in the haystack because he knew my mother would not go near the pigpen. I had known his secret hiding place for a while, but I knew better than to tell my mother. I had one of my own. As I was looking for my mother, I noticed that the front gate was open. I walked towards it and looked out to see if she was in the street. I saw her. She was walking back with more beer — her face sprinkled with third degree burns — as if nothing had happened. I raced back into the house. I did not want to take any chance that this would be the day she would take her anger out on me. I ran into the closet with a blanket and a pillow. I fell asleep for a few minutes, but woke up after having a nightmare. I think that was around the time when my nightmares began.

I woke up, left the closet and slowly walked to the living room where I saw my mother passed out on the sofa, lights on and doors open. I don't remember why that night I decided not to sleep on the floor next to her. I think the burns on her face scared me. I went another route. I went outside get all of my puppies and bring them inside to sleep with me. At twelve o'clock at night, there I was, bringing four-month old puppies into the house. Not just one or two, but all nine were destined to sleep in my room with me that night. I brought in the first four through the door and soon found that every time I would open the door to go bring another, one would leave. I would go chase that one down, open the door and bring it in, just to have another little sucker escape. I came up with another plan. I would not open the door. Instead, I would jump through the window and bring them in that way. The last few I brought in through the window. It was a taxing task but in the end, I had all of them in my bedroom. I played with them for a while until somehow I fell asleep.

It felt like I had been asleep for just minutes when I was suddenly woken up by my mother's screams. She came into the room and saw all the dogs there. I don't know how I did not wake to their squirming; I must have been exhausted, but my mother's screams sure woke me up. She was very upset because the puppies had pooped everywhere. They had chewed on my shoes and toys, they had made quite a mess. I quickly got up, got dressed, ignored the ugly sight of my mother's burned face, ate cereal and left for school. I came home that day thinking I would be scolded for having brought the dogs in, but the opposite happened. My mother was feeling guilty for what she did not remember had happened the night before. From the unmistakable signs on her face, she knew it had not been good, so she was nice to me. She had cleaned the house and not mentioned anything to me, we did not even talk about what had happened to her face. We all pretended that her face was not burned. That day, I began to see my animals not only as friends but as my protectors as well. They were there for me when I was scared or when I just needed company.

Finally, there were the cows. My stepfather would buy the cows as calves and we would feed them and care for them until they were big enough to kill. My stepfather would shoot them, cut up the meat and sell them. They, too, were destined to have a bullet go through their foreheads. My stepfather said that shooting them in the forehead would make them die instantly and cause the meat to remain softer and juicier. I don't know how true that is, but that's how it was done.

There are three strong memories I have of the cows. The first is being able to feed them with bottles when they were little. The calves made loud distinctive moos when they were hungry. We would prepare huge bottles by mixing water with milk powder to make the formula. Then we would hold up the bottle for them until they had sucked all the formula. I can still remember the smell of the formula. It smelled exactly like baby formula. During the times my older sister was home, she would get upset because the calves would wake us up early. By five o'clock they were hungry and mooing at our bedroom window. My mother would have us go out and feed them. I often looked at a picture I have that was taken on one of those days when I was lucky enough to have my sister home in which she was feeding a calf.

There was also that time when one of the cows came into our house. We had left the back door open, and this cow, the biggest one out of five, decided to wander in. Both my mother and I tried for what seemed like an hour to get him out. He would wander from the kitchen to the bedroom, then to the bathroom and the living room. Finally, after an exhausting feat, we managed to herd him out of the front door. Unfortunately, he sprained his ankle on the way out and for the next few weeks of his life, he walked with a limp. He, too, met his day with a gun.

I remember the cows well because I suffered a very painful injury with one of them. My mother had begun her drinking for the day and was not quite at the point of violence yet. It was early in the afternoon, two or three o'clock maybe. We were outside doing some chores. The cows were very friendly. They always knew they would be taken care of. This particular day, a cow walked up to my mother probably hoping to get some food, when my mother came up with what seemed like a bright idea. She decided to sit me facing backwards on the cow. There I was, sitting on this cow facing his butt and holding on to my mother's shirt. I was begging for her not to let me go. I was mortified that she would and that I would end up falling down. I had known better than to get on the cows because my stepfather had warned me that they were not trained to have people sit on them. "They are not for riding," he said. After a few minutes sitting on this cow, my worst fear came true.

Even though my mother repeatedly promised that she would not let me go, and though I begged her endlessly, she let me go. I fought hard not to let go of her shirt, but she had already removed my grip on her. As I jerked to regain a grip on her shirt, the cow decided to take off. And not just walk, but run. It ran like it was being chased by some ferocious and hungry lion, not caring one bit that I was sitting on its back, facing backward. It ran a few feet and by the grace of God, I fell off right before I hit a large branch of a tree. Had I not fallen at the moment I did, the back of my head would have hit the branch that was sticking out from the tree trunk, and I could have ended up with a severe concussion, or even death. I fell a few feet and landed on my butt, my tailbone hitting the ground really hard. The fall was extremely painful as I was a skinny little thing. All I kept thinking was how could she have let me go. My mother ran to me as I started to cry in pain. My back was hurting and so were my legs. I had damaged something, I was not sure what. All I knew was that I could not get up. My mother carried me inside the house and asked me if she should call the ambulance. She followed her question with, "They will take you away from me if I do." In pain, I said no. I did not want to be taken away from her. I don't know what happened after that or how I was taken care of but I know that she did not take me to the doctor's office to have me checked for injuries.

For the next few days, walking was difficult, especially stepping onto the curb. That was extremely painful. When I walked anywhere I always dreaded having to step off or onto the sidewalk because of the excruciating pain in my back. A few years back, I had a back spasm. One of a few that I would continue to have. I went to the chiropractor and I now know that that incident caused my spinal cord to compress — a part of my backbone had been crushed.

Whenever I see cows, that's my first thought. The memory of the day my mother decided I would ride a cow. I don't harbor any resentment towards my mother or cows, I know that it was neither one's fault. My mother was ill and the cow was just being a cow. Animals clearly had an impact on my life. That is why even today I cannot live without at least a fish in my home. So far I have had goats, rabbits, guinea pigs, birds, turtles, cats, dogs, mice and hamsters. I truly believe that they are angels that come to us when we most need them. They come to us disguised as animals.

My days weren't always spent with my animals. I enjoyed insects as well. Spiders and ants fascinated me. Often, I would sit and watch the ants at work. I loved to see such dedication. They would come in and out of the hole they had dug in the ground, on a mission, to find food. I noticed different sized ants would scurry in and out. Some would go far and come back with food; others would stay near the entrance. I quickly figured out that those were the protectors, the guards. Their job was to make sure no intruders entered their home. They were really good at it too, since I never saw any intruders near the area. The ones that ventured far from the hole were the worker ants. They would run from one place to another as if time was of the essence. I think it was because they were supposed to be in their home by evening so they had to go and find food as fast as possible. I admired the workers. They would carry food that was really big and heavy. I remember one carry a whole cooked pinto bean back into the hole one time. That was amazing. I also noticed that their work was not mindless, isolated drivel, they were really nice to each other. As they encountered other ants on the way, they would greet each other by stopping to touch antennae. That was fascinating to see. When an ant died on the field, there was always one that would carry it back into the hole. I always wondered why. I would make up stories about how they would have a funeral ceremony inside. I don't know what they do with their dead friends. But I still want to think they would bury them somewhere inside those underground tunnels.

One day after observing, watching them come in and out, I paused and wondered what would happen if the entrance to their home were blocked. What would happen if the hole were covered for some reason? Would they make another one? They probably would, and I wanted to see it for myself. I wanted to see them actually dig another hole. So, in my bright nine-year old mind, I covered up the hole with nothing other than my finger. Before my finger even touched the dirt, I swear I had about twenty huge, red soldier ants curled up around my pointer finger with their stingers firmly stabbed inside.

They must have jumped to my finger because I know for sure my finger never touched the ground.

I can't begin to describe the pain I felt. I screamed as hard as my nine-year old lungs could muster and ran as fast as I could inside the house, bringing all twenty ants with me on my finger. My mother heard my screams and ran toward me at the same time I was running toward her. Between sobs, I tried to explain what had happened, but my finger spoke for itself. She did not scold me; she just grabbed a pair of tweezers and began to pull the ants out, one by one. I cried the whole time. She casually asked, "What the hell were you thinking?" (in Spanish, of course). Thank goodness she was not drinking that day; otherwise, all twenty ants would have stayed stuck to my finger until the next day. Needless to say, I stayed away from ants ever since. Ants are dangerous.

My days at home were spent being surrounded by animals. These animals taught me many lessons. Especially in care-taking. Caring for all of them took work and money. This was also the time when I learned the meaning of the colloquial phrase "trash picking." Literally, we went through trash cans to get food, but not because we needed it. My stepfather had a decent job and my mother received government assistance, so we had food — if and when my mother bought food. If she did not, my stepfather would bring stuff to eat from the local market, Santa Fe Market. I remember this market because we often frequented it; it was the place my mother bought groceries and her beer and her cigarettes. This was the place where my mother and stepfather would take my older sister and me to scavenge the trash bins in the back alley, late at night, to collect food. We would go through the bins and take out what vegetables and fruits were still good, I used to be surprised how much food was still good yet was being thrown out. The store would throw away the produce that had slight damage to it, so we would bag lettuce, tomatoes, cabbage, pears, apples, you name it, and we would take them home.

My sister and I were in charge of digging through the bin and showing the food to either my mom or stepdad. They would then signal to us whether it was good to take home or not. We would often harvest loaves of bread and sweet bread, slightly damaged cans, and boxes of cereal. When we would find these things, it felt like finding treasure. My mom would become really happy. We would go home smelly and sweaty, but with bountiful bags of food from the big trash bins.

Once at home, my mother would sort through the food and leave the best for our family. The rest would go as food for the animals. The pigs, cows and chickens would have a feast. I was really thankful that none of my friends ever saw me picking through the trash bins. Talk about humiliation. I would have been a complete and total outcast (more than I already was) with an added label of "trash picker."

Chapter 8

Is He Dead?

The early part of third grade was when everything changed for me. A new family had moved into the house to the left of us. It was actually a church, but behind it there was a home that housed the pastor of that church and his family. Up until that moment I had never gone to church. My mother was not a big believer in religion, and God was rarely mentioned, so I knew nothing about the Bible. She did, on occasion, mention angels to me and that we were born with ten and would lose one each time we were bad. I truly believed it and could not bear the thought of counting how many times I had done something wrong and lost one. To begin with, I had probably already lost five when I killed those baby chicks. And then there was that time in first grade when a boy was making fun of me and I stabbed him with a semi-sharpened pencil. I only made a small mark and did not draw blood, but it was wrong and I knew I hurt him. I must have lost two more then. When the "Church family" as I called them moved there, I was more curious about them than I had been about the previous family because they had children, two girls. One was older than me, the other one a bit younger, a year or two I'd say. They came over to introduce themselves one day and invited us to go to church. My mother had not been drinking that day and politely declined the offer.

That did not stop them from trying to get us to attend their church. Once in a while, the little girls would come over and ask me to go to church with them especially on certain days when they would have events likes fairs or workshops for kids. I was usually allowed to go when my mom was either in a good mood or drinking but not yet drunk. I think she figured it was a good way to get me out of her hair especially on the days she was drinking. This is because on her drinking days, I would try to stop her by hiding her beer or dumping it in the sink. So she had no problem with me going to church.

At the church, the adults would usher us into a small room with other children. There were children of all ages. We would sit on the floor and we would sing songs and learn about stuff — God stuff. I called it stuff because most of the time, I was lost. I had no clue what they were talking about. First of all, my English was not very good. I was an English Language Learner, meaning that my first language was Spanish, and I only learned English at school. As it was, I was already behind at school so most of the level of language they used were foreign to me. They used big words and terms that I did not understand.

The family who had moved there was white. Caucasian is the correct term, and so was most of the congregation. I think I was the only Hispanic kid there. It did not matter to me, though. I was happy to get away from my house and to be a part of a family. Not to mention I loved the cookies and punch. They always had cookies and punch. Not that my house did not have food, but I think I did not eat often enough. As time went on, I began to spend more time at the church with the other kids. I noticed that the girls would invite me more often. I know now that they were doing it to get me out of my home. They knew about my situation so they would come to get me when my mother was drinking. I also started sleeping over on those days. I loved it. I did not have to go into my closet on those bad days. I could go over to their house and play. One night they were not home, so they could not come over and save me from what I had to experience. It was one of the worst days of my life.

It started like any other bad day. By eight o'clock at night, the violence between my mother and my stepfather had escalated. My mother had hit and slapped my stepfather and, in turn, my mother had been punched in the face. Once I saw that, I went straight to my room to hide in the closet. As I was about to close the door behind me, I heard my mother yell at my stepfather that she was going to get the gun he kept under his pillow and kill him. I knew that once drunk, my mother was capable of anything.

My stepfather had always kept a gun under his pillow for protection. It was always loaded and he had extra bullets in his dresser drawer. My mother would always ask him, when she was sober, to remove the gun from there. She said it was a safety issue, she did not want me to get to it. That night, after many hours of drinking and many beers emptied, she threatened my father with the gun. This had never happened before. I was torn between staying in the closet or going out to the living room to try and stop the situation. I decided that I was not about to let her shoot him. I opened the closet door and ran outside just in time to see my mother pointing the gun, finger on the trigger, ready to shoot my stepfather in the stomach. My heart stopped and I felt sick to my stomach. It was at that moment that my survival instinct kicked in. Instead of standing there like a deer in headlights, I yelled and screamed for her to stop, but she would not shift her aim away from him. She did not even turn to look at me. But I know she heard me because her response to was, "Do you see, Alicia, what he has done to me? I am tired of this. I'm going to kill him." My mother had a black eye. What she could not see was that she had scratched and punched him first. She was always the one to hit first. She was just as guilty as he was in this whole mess. "Stay back!" she yelled at me. I knew there was no changing her mind and I knew that I did not have enough time to run back into the closet. I turned my body to face the window, pulled the curtain aside and looked out into the eerie darkness. I knew she was going to pull the trigger; she was going to kill him and I could not do anything. As I stared out the window of our neighborhood street, I began to leave this world and enter into my imaginary world. The world I had created in the closet, only this time I was not in the closet.

As I began to focus on the streets and the cars parked outside, turning them into beautiful creeks in the middle of a lush forest with vibrant colors of red, green, gold and blue slowly beginning to emerge, and sounds of violence fading into sweet, loving chirps, my stepfather's screams brought me back. I turned and my mother was still holding the gun, her hand shaking, but still had a tight grip on it. The barrel of the gun was touching my stepfather's stomach, she had positioned herself, ready to shoot. That person holding the gun was not my mother; the evil in her eyes was not her. I knew that in her right mind she would never do that. As I stared into my mother's eyes, I could hear my stepfather yelling "Shoot me, shoot me if you want." At that point I envisioned her pulling the trigger, firing a fatal shot and tearing a hole through his flesh. A deep hole that would ooze with blood as it poured out of his body. I envisioned him falling and blood splattering everywhere while my mother stood there, holding the gun. Blood on the walls, blood on the floor, and splatters of blood on my face. My next thought was that she would shoot me too, and then herself. A murder suicide, they call it. That horrible line of thinking was shattered when he once again dared her to shoot him.

With her finger on the trigger, she did what I had seen in my vision — she pulled the trigger. I closed my eyes but all I heard was the hollow snap of the gun. I quickly opened my eyes to see what happened. I expected him screaming with blood everywhere, but there was not any of that. My stepfather quickly yanked the gun away from her and walked out the front door, leaving her and me in shock. I had just witnessed a miracle.

Earlier that day, my stepfather had been cleaning his gun as he usually did once a week when some friends dropped by for a visit. This did not give him time to reload his gun as he usually did, so he figured he would reload the gun at a later time. He forgot to reload it, and that was the day my mother decided to pull the trigger. My mother, dumbfounded, turned around and walked into her room and fell asleep. I went to bed late that night, maybe in the closet or near my mother — wherever she had passed out. Not in the nice, warm, safe home in which the pastor and his family lived. I wished I could have slept in his house that night.

I went to bed thinking about their soft, plush beds covered with pink and white comforters that had designs of dolls on them. I thought about the fresh baked cookies and punch their mom made. During that year, I would stay over at their house from time to time. During many of those times, my mom would wind up on their front door, yelling and screaming, wanting for me to go home. Every time she would come to get me, I would pray that she would leave. Each time, the pastor would speak with her in his broken Spanish and she would then let me stay. I would get to sleep comfortably. Just not this night.

Chapter 9

I Stole the Stickers

Every morning after sleeping at the pastor's home, I would wake up with knots in my stomach, not wanting to go home. I was angry and sad, but most of all, I was jealous. I was jealous that these two girls could stay while I had to leave. I became so angry that one day I took out that anger while riding my bike. I was riding in the church parking lot. There were no services that day, so there weren't any cars. Their family was not home. I rode around for a while when I noticed that the door leading to the room where all the children would sing songs and eat snacks was slightly open. I dropped my bike and slowly walked to the door and pulled it open. I took a few steps inside and I looked around to see if anyone was there. Not a soul in sight. I walked inside with no specific intentions but to walk around. I entered the children's room and saw the desk where the teacher kept the rewards for the kids. She kept pencils and stickers in there. I had seen her pull them out from the desk many times. I stepped closer and carefully opened the drawer. I knew that if someone walked in, I would be in trouble. Not to mention the shame and embarrassment I would feel, for I knew better than to be inside without permission.

At nine years old, my heart knew right from wrong. I knew it was wrong to open the drawer without permission, and what I was about to do next was far worse. Inside the drawer, I saw a pack of stickers. Lots of packs actually. I thought about it for a moment and then decided I was going to steal them.

I grabbed a few packs, stuck them into my pockets, and like the thief I had become, ran out the door, hopped onto my bike and took off. I took the stickers out of spite and jealousy. I figured that they had a lot of good stuff already, including a good home and loving parents, so taking stickers would not be a big deal. What I did not realize was at that moment, I had opened my heart up to a new world of shame. For the next twenty years I would have to live with the shame and guilt of having stolen a bunch of stupid stickers just because I was jealous. And not just from anywhere, but from people who had been kind to me. I had to truly forgive myself for that one. Never again did I ever steal anything without knowing the aftertaste of such an act; the remorse that I felt in my heart for what I had done was too painful to ever take on so lightly again. I knew that I had made a choice to feel pain. That was a huge lesson. At age nine, I learned that I could make choices that could either cause me pain or happiness. For the first time I knew I had power over my life.

I went back the next Sunday to that same room. I remember feeling so guilty that I could not look the teacher in the eye. It had been a mistake to even show up. I felt so uncomfortable. I remember she said something about the missing stickers. I knew in my heart she knew it was me; she never asked me though. She did not have to. My heart showed through my face. I never went back to Sunday school; instead, I made every excuse as to why I could not go. When the little girls came to get me, I would either say my stomach was hurting or I would not answer the door. I would tell my mom to tell them I was asleep. Talk about more angels leaving. I think I was down to my last one after stealing and lying. I did not learn much about God at Sunday school as I did not understand much what they were saying. It did teach me my greatest lesson. That even though I was young, I was not powerless in this life — I could control my destiny. This, I believe, is the BIGGEST and most POWERFUL lesson any child could learn. I did not see that family again because shortly after that encounter, I was sent to a foster home.

Chapter 10

The Neverending Story

The events that changed my life for the better started one night after my mother had been drinking. I decided I wanted to bring my dogs into the house. It was getting dark, my mom would not go to sleep early, and I had school the next day. It was about nine o'clock at night, and I was jumping in and out of my window, bringing my dogs, which were now a little older, into the house. I was about to jump out the window, when my mother grabbed me by my ponytail, so that I wouldn't jump off. I had not noticed, but the church family had been outside sitting in their front yard, which had a view of our back yard and my window. They witnessed my mother pulling me by the hair and I guess by this point they felt compelled to do something. I did not know what that was until the next day. After attempting to bring my dogs in and being unsuccessful, I fell asleep in my closet. I woke up in the middle of the night to screams and dishes being thrown and broken. Off and on I would sleep. I knew I had to get sleep because I had school the next day. Darkness often seemed so long when I was waiting for school.

The next morning, wearing the same clothes, I boarded the yellow bus to school. That day, a lady came into the classroom, and asked me to follow her to the office. I wondered, was I in trouble? Did I forget something? Had my mom come to pick me up? She would do that sometimes. She would feel guilty about putting me through such harsh situations, so she would take me out of school and take me shopping. She would buy me candy or a toy. I know she meant well, but I hated it. I hated her doing this because I knew it was a pattern. She would apologize, buy me something, and then do it again.

As I approached the office, I saw a group of people standing around talking. As soon as they saw me, they stopped to look at me. It was one of those awkward moments when you know people have stopped talking because the conversation was about you. They led me to a room and left me alone with another lady. This lady looked me over and began to ask me questions. She asked if my mother would hit me. "No," was my answer. She asked if I would get hit in my face and if that was why I had black under my eyes. "No," I responded again. She did not know that the dark circles were from the lack of sleep. They were, however, bad enough to be confused with bruised eyes, from being hit. I appreciated that she took the time to explain why she was there, in language that I could understand. She said she had been called because people had seen my mom hit me and pull my hair. She said the neighbors saw it and reported it, so she was there to make sure I was all right. Wow — had I just heard her say she wanted to make sure I was all right? It felt strange to have someone say they cared about my well-being. They were there for me. She continued asking questions about my mother and her drinking. I wanted to tell her everything. I wanted to tell her that I was scared, that I could not sleep. I wanted to tell her that my mother had pointed a gun to my stepfather's stomach and pulled the trigger, that she tried to burn him with hot cooking oil, and that she would regularly be beaten. I especially wanted to tell her about my sisters. Could she help my sisters? I wanted to tell her about "God" and how he had helped me when I prayed. But would she believe me? I also wanted to tell her about the quarters — lots of quarters.

After I felt that prayer had stopped working and God no longer heard my pleas to have my parents stop fighting, I came up with an idea. I decided to pay God for his help. Don't ask me where I got this idea because I don't remember. All I know is that I would steal quarters from my mom and stepdad and I would go bury them outside, beside our house. I would look up at the sun because that's where I thought God lived and would ask for my parents to stop fighting. The first time I dug a hole to bury a quarter, I made a small hole, stuck the quarter in and covered it up. That night my mother drank but did not fight. I was astonished. Paying God for helping me had worked, so I did it again the next night. And the next. Eventually, it got to the point where

54

I thought God wanted more money because after a few one-quarter nights, life went back to its dysfunctional self. As a result, I began to bury two quarters and then three until finally, day after day and week after week I began to run out of quarters. I figured God was just too busy or he did not need the money. Somewhere on that lot on Rush Street in El Monte, there are tons of quarters still buried. I wanted to tell the lady all of this so badly. Instead, all my answers were but one word. "Yes" or "No."

I did not return to my classroom. Instead, she drove me home and on the way there, silence filled the air. An awkward silence. She did explain to me that I needed to pack some clothes because I was going to another family. It did not quite hit me. I heard bits and pieces of what she said. I heard, "going . . . family . . . clothes." When I got home, my mother was waiting at the door. She led me to the bedroom where she already had clothes packed in a bag and helped me change into nicer clothes. She cried the whole time. Tears streaming down her face. Tears unlike any other I had seen her shed. Her usual tears were of anger and hate. This time they were tears of sadness. Still up to that point I had no idea what was going on. All I heard was, *"te quiero mucho."* Her last words were I love you. Had she said I love you? That completely caught me off guard. Now I was even more bewildered. She told me she loved me. She had never said those words before. Something must have been wrong. She led me back into the living room where the social worker was waiting for me. She took my bag and led me to the car. Somehow, I felt like I had done something wrong, I just did not know what.

We drove for what seemed like hours. Again, awkward silence all the way. I did not know what to say or ask and I think she felt the same way. We were strangers, so conversation was not what I wanted. Especially when I did not understand what was going on.

When we arrived at the foster home, she explained that I would stay with a nice family who had other children who were going through family problems. I looked at her and then turned my head to see the house where I would be staying. It was a nice looking house. Nicer than where I lived. She rang the doorbell and the door opened. The husband and wife greeted us. "You're going to be staying with them for a while," was all I remember her saying. The lady left, and the couple ushered me in. They showed me around and introduced me to their 12-year old son and their daughter who must have been around my age. They showed me my room; I would be sharing it with their daughter. There were two beds, I would have the one to the left and farthest from the door. I asked if I could lie down and they said yes. In my exhaustion, I fell asleep. They woke me up for dinner and I had a few bites. I missed my mom and my home. I was in a house with strangers — nice strangers, but strangers nonetheless. I did not know if I would see my mom or my sisters again. What were they doing and what were they thinking? Were they thinking about me? Were they worried about me? I needed to somehow let them know I was safe. After brushing my teeth and changing into my pajamas, I fell asleep.

I woke up to the sound of their daughter crying. She was kicking and screaming at the top of her lungs. The mom and dad rushed in and held her down. She was having a seizure. I freaked out. She was shaking uncontrollably and had wet her bed. I looked on in disbelief. After this episode, I turned around and pretended to be asleep. The next morning, another lady came to ask about their daughter. The little girl was also a foster child and the lady was a social worker, so I was not the only one. She asked a few questions and then the conversation turned to me. "She needs to go to school. Maybe it will be good for her," said the lady. The couple asked me if I would like to go to school or wait. I knew better than to say go to school. I was not about to go to another new place where I did not know anyone. "Not right now," I said. They were kind enough not to force me to go that week.

Later that afternoon, while the family was in the backyard playing, I tried to sneak in a phone call to my mother. I gave them the excuse that I needed to drink some water. So I inched my way to the kitchen where they kept the telephone. I pretended to get some water, all the while keeping an eye out to make sure no one was coming. I was nervous and afraid I would be caught. I quickly grabbed the phone and dialed my home number. No one answered. I hung up and dialed several more times. Each time, no one answered. My home phone number was the only number I knew, so I could not call anyone else. I was heartbroken. Had they forgotten me already? Did they not care what happened to me? I did not get caught, but somehow my foster parents found out I was using the phone, so it was taken off the kitchen wall that day. I was not able to call again.

A week later, my social worker came to see me. She had come to explain that I would be picked up by a yellow bus and taken to the Children's Court. I did not understand what she was saying other than the part that I would see my mother. I would see my mom there and I could tell the judge everything. That's all I heard. I nodded my head in agreement because I did not know what else to say. I was happy however that I would get to see my mom. I wanted to tell her to come get me and that I missed her very much. The next day the yellow bus arrived. The driver got off and checked my name off the list. I had been waiting in the living room for a while, anxiety slowly creeping in, so seeing him at the door was a relief. I was excited. Excited to see my mom. I hopped on the bus and looked around for a good seat. It was mostly empty except for about three kids who were a bit older. They were quietly sitting on their seats and didn't seem to care that I was getting on the bus because they did not turn to look at me. They too, seemed lost in this whole thing. I was a quiet person, so making friends would not be high on my list of things to do on the bus. I sat on the third seat behind the bus driver, by myself. I scooted as far as I could so that I could see out the window. The bus driver started the bus and off we went.

We arrived at McLaren Hall shortly thereafter. I was the last foster child to be picked up at home. Upon pulling up into the driveway, I noticed that we had stopped in front of a tall, electric metal gate. The whole building was a pale blue and had lots of windows. The section we were entering into had bars on windows and a double gate that separated the outside world. I wasn't sure where I was. I thought that we had arrived at the place where I would see my mother. My mind began to race, "Is this where my mother was being held? Had she done such a horrible thing that she had to be behind bars?"

The first metal gate rose as we approached and the yellow bus went in. Then, it stopped because the second gate had not opened immediately. The first gate closed completely behind us and it took a few seconds for the gate in front of us to open. Those seconds were scary. We were there for what seemed like a long time, trapped between two tall, thick metal gates. "How bad is this place if we had to be locked in here?"

The second gate opened and the yellow bus proceeded to the entrance of the building. The bus driver opened the door of the bus and walked outside. I could see him standing at the building entrance with a notepad and pen. One by one kids started coming out. They were of many cultural backgrounds: African American, Caucasian and Hispanic. I don't remember seeing any Asians. They ranged in ages from seven to seventeen. They came onto the bus in such a loud and disruptive manner. Some were yelling at other kids or jokingly hitting each other, a few were quiet. The commotion frightened me, so I did the only thing I knew to do in a scary situation. I looked out the window and imagined myself back in the forest with all my animal friends. It worked because I don't remember the rest of the ride to the courthouse.

I remember walking into a room that resembled a classroom. It had a long table with crayons and paper; there was a section with toys, building blocks, dolls, and puzzles. There was a television and some chairs. By that time all the children had been separated. The older ones went to another room, and I think the ones I was with were twelve and under. I simply looked around. Shortly after that, they announced it was snack time. I was still wondering when I would see my mother. Nobody explained the process or where we were. I needed some explanation. I wanted some adult to answer the questions I had. "Where was I and when would I see my mother?" Did adults not understand that we had concerns? They must have thought that because we were children, we wouldn't understand. I was nine and I would understand.

As we gathered around the table to eat our snack, a cookie and milk, I took some time to pick out a good spot — a spot where nobody would notice me. I picked a quarter of the way down the side of the table. If I chose the middle area to sit at, I would have been noticed from both sides; if I chose the ends I would have been noticed, too, but between the middle and the end, I would blend in perfectly. It was a long rectangular table, with lots of kids. Surely no one would notice me.

My theory was wrong. As soon as I was handed my milk and cookie, an older girl, she must have been twelve, came over to where I was sitting while the teacher was not looking and took my cookie. She caught me by surprise. She looked at me and said, "If you say anything, I will beat you up." I was freaked out, so of course, as hungry as I was and as much as I wanted that cookie, I did not say a word. I drank my milk quietly while the others just glanced at me, eating their cookies, all the while I was struggling to hold back my tears.

I finished my milk, got up, and sat on a chair in front of the big TV where a movie was to be shown. I waited for the other kids to finish their snack so the movie could start. I did not worry about picking a special (safe) spot since I had failed miserably at the first attempt to hide from the other kids. I did, however, chose a seat near the teacher. This time I wanted someone to watch over me. The kids finished their snacks, a lady turned off the lights and the movie started. All the kids were quiet.

The title quickly caught my attention: The Neverending Story. The movie took me to a place that I so desperately needed to go at that moment. A few minutes into the movie, I realized that it resembled my life. It centered on a boy whose mother had died and who was neglected by his depressed father. He also had to deal with bullying at school. While running away from a group of bullies one day, he hid in a bookstore and began to read The NeverEnding Story. He got so caught up in it that he ended up stealing the book. Bastian, the boy, then hid in his school's attic where he proceeded to read the rest of the story. As he dove deeper into it, he had been magically brought into the story and thus became part of it and was now one of the characters. I was immediately drawn into the movie because of the problems Bastian faced. He, like me, had been neglected and bullied. And just like me, he had found solace and safety in his school and books.

I continued to watch and became even more captivated when Bastian magically entered the world he was reading about. He had entered the magical kingdom called Fantasia. Fantasia was this beautiful bright city with lots of animals and beautiful forests. It reminded me of my own make-believe world. The one I would enter when hiding in my closet when things at home were bad. The movie had a beautiful and loving dragon, Falkor, that flew Bastian everywhere. He was a Luck Dragon, it had the head of a dog and a furry body that resembled a dragon.

I decided at that moment that the next time I entered my imaginary world, I would create a Luck Dragon. I would create one that looked just like Falkor and he would fly me everywhere. Unfortunately, the kingdom that Bastian had entered was slowly being destroyed because the child empress was ill. The fact that the characters were children about my age and that the magical kingdom reminded me of my own made me feel at ease with all that was going on in this cold and empty room in the courthouse. After a while of watching the movie, I too felt as though I had become part of the movie and the things that were happening in the room and the fact that some bully had stolen my cookie earlier were things I no longer worried about.

After Bastian entered the book he was reading, he met the empress and she asked him to help her rebuild the city once it was saved. She asked him to use his imagination to help him and this led Bastian to have many adventures of his own in his new world. This made a lot of sense to me. However, Bastian needed to go back to reality, to his real life. But he must first find the only thing he can wish for without losing himself. He must find his own true will. Bastian not only found his true will, which is love, but he also found that he became stronger and more courageous as he confronted life and its problems instead of running from them.

I was blessed to have seen the movie to the end because not only did it take my mind off what was happening, but I learned that sometimes difficult things happen to us and we must face them instead of hiding from them. At age nine, I understood the moral of the story, the lesson it taught us. I felt better; I felt a sense of strength and courage. I wanted to be like Bastian that day. I wanted to be brave enough to face the Children's Court.

Right when the movie ended, my name was called by the teacher. It was my turn to enter the courtroom. She held my hand and led me through some double doors. As I went into the next room, the first person I saw was my older sister. She was sitting at a table just the way I had seen in people who had to go to a courtroom on TV. There was a man next to her, the court appointed lawyer. The minute our eyes met, we both felt a sense of relief. Sitting on the far left at a different table was my mother. The minute she saw me enter the courtroom, she began to cry uncontrollably. That was the second time I had seen my mother cry with so much despair. The first time was when she said goodbye to me the day I was removed from our home. I felt so sorry for her. Then my sister began to cry as well. Sadness overtook me and tears began to fall.

I was told I had to go straight to the stand. It was a tall brown box area with a chair. The judge was next to me on a higher platform. The lady told me that the judge needed to ask me some questions. With tears in my eyes and a desperate longing to hug my mother and my sister, I followed the lady's instructions. I was sitted in the stand and glanced into the seating area. There were many people waiting their turn. Mothers and fathers and foster parents I assumed. I also saw a police officer. He was standing near the door, making sure all was safe. It was an odd place — a place I knew major decisions were made. A powerful place. I could feel it. My observation of the room was broken when the judge asked me the first question. I don't remember what the first ones were, but I do know several more questions followed. In my loudest voice I answered each one truthfully. Especially when he asked if I wanted to be with my mother. I said, "Yes." He asked if I wanted to go home with my sister. I looked over at her, her eyes red from crying and I said, "Yes." I wanted my family. I wanted to go home with them. I was quickly escorted out of the room and back into the room with the other children.

My next memory is of me unpacking my suitcase a few days later at my sister's new house. I was declared a ward of the state and my nineteen-year old sister was my guardian. She had taken on the huge responsibility of being the guardian for both my sixteen-year old sister and me. I so admire her and love her for making it so I did not have to stay anywhere else. She loved us enough to stop her life and take us in. She would raise us for a year while my mother completed her mandatory rehabilitation at a center for alcoholics. My mother had been sent to a home where she would learn to live life without drinking. In order for her to get regain custody of us she would have to prove she had been sober for a year. It was exciting to be back with my family, my sisters. It was also odd because it was a new home in a new city: East Los Angeles. My sister had rented a two-bedroom apartment where my older sister, her boyfriend, my middle sister and I would live. I had to enroll in a new school.

Chapter 11

A New Beginning

I finished third grade at this new school. I liked this school. It was close to our new home and the teachers were nice. I became a little more sociable because nobody knew my history. I had a clean slate. I could start all over, and I would not tell anyone what had happened to me. I was not going to allow anyone to judge me or to make fun of me. My life was perfect. My older sister would drop me off at school and pick me up after school. The unfortunate thing about this was that she did not have time to go back to college. She had to make sure we were taken care of. Things were fine for a while until life decided it wanted to test my strength again. A few girls decided they were going to bully me. I guess I was a bully magnet. Quiet and shy girls are their prey. I guess bullies felt they could pick on the weak ones.

I went home that day and told my sister. She was furious. The next day, she was waiting for me at the gate right after school. "So who is this that is bothering you?" she asked. I pointed a group of fifth-grade girls. She walked over to them, and cornered them between a fence. She looked at each one and said, "If you continue to bother my sister, I will come back and it's not going to be pretty. You'd better leave her alone." Her tone of voice was one that it scared even me. I was so proud of my sister. I stood tall and brave and had the look of, "Yeah, go ahead and mess with me." Needless to say, they never as much as even looked at me again. The rest of third grade was a breeze.

My mother had been sent to a nice two-story rehabilitation center for alcoholics. This place would help her to stop drinking. The ladies who were also there trying to get better were really friendly, and so were the workers. I was able to visit my mother some weekends and in turn she would come over to our house on some weekends. Holidays were a lot of fun. I would spend them with her at her rehab house. It was fun because holidays were not that special for us before. I don't recall any fun events during Easter, Saint Patrick's Day or any other holiday aside from Christmas. Yet at the rehabilitation house, they always had parties for every occasion. And not just any party but full blown, tons of decorations and food parties. One Easter, I got all dressed up and spent it with her in the rehab home. They had many goodies like cake, candy, punch and sandwiches. They had decorated the lush backyard with Easter decorations, and they hid eggs for the egg hunt. All the kids were given baskets in which to place the eggs they would find. Even though I was close to ten, I was still so much a child at heart. A child who wanted to experience fun stuff — the stuff of life that I had never experienced before.

When the egg hunt started, I searched and searched for those eggs. I was on a mission. To find as many eggs as possible. I was so happy that day. On days when there were no parties at the rehab center, we would gather around in the living room and watch television. Sometimes, my mother and I would take a walk to the corner liquor store to buy candies. Her favorite were the Chick-O-Sticks. I would get chocolates. She'd ask me about school and home and she would tell me stories about her new home. The conversations were strange. I had never had conversations with my mom like this before. Before rehab, she would never ask me about school. She would not ask about home-work either. We basically never talked. This season was when she and I began to get to know each other in a different way. In a true mother-daughter way. Before this, I knew my mother only in two ways: her being drunk and violent or her feeling guilty and being overly nice. There was no in-between. These two extremes were very difficult to deal with. But now, she was consistent. She was her true self.

On the weekends, we would go to the movies, eat out, or shop in Down-town L.A. She would take me to the toy district and buy me a toy or two. This time buying toys was different. She was buying me toys not because she felt guilty about being drunk the day before, but because I loved the toy district. We would walk from one store to another, each one magically filled with all kinds of different toys. We always took the bus which was fun, too. Taking the bus would remind me of the days before my mother began drinking heavily when we lived in that green house in East LA. My mother would clean the house of an elderly woman every other day and since my mother did not drive, we took the bus everywhere. The bus stopped right in front of the old lady's house. We would get off, go inside and while my mother cooked and cleaned for her, I would play with the lady's dog.

The dog's name was Lobo (Spanish for wolf) and he sure looked like a wolf. He was a sweet dog and we would play together all the time. We had bonded so much that when my mother would feed him his crunchy food, I would wait for my mother to leave the laundry room where she would put his food and I would get on all fours and eat with him. Yes, out of the same bowl. It did not happen often, but admittedly sometimes I'd share a snack. Mind you, I was only four years old. Lord knows that that dog was patient with me. Sharing food is something dogs normally don't do. I think he understood that I was only four. He was a smart dog. I stopped sharing his food when my mother caught me eating out of his bowl one day. She was upset, of course. I don't know what she said, but I am sure it was her tone of voice that made me realize what I was doing was not right, so I stopped. I did not get away without being bitten though. One day I was outside playing with a balloon my mother had inflated for me. When my mom went inside the house to finish her housekeeping duties, I began rubbing the balloon on Lobo's back. The static must have shocked him and he reacted defensively, because the next thing I knew, my neck was in his mouth. My mother heard me scream and she ran outside in time to see him let me go. Even though Lobo had very sharp teeth, he did not leave a mark on me. Not even a scratch. Talk about a miracle in the works. I must have had my angels with me that day. All eleven.

After my mom finished her chores, we would leave the house and wait for the bus to ride home. One time we were sitting on the bench waiting for the bus when suddenly my mother got up. She walked towards a tree that was surrounded by many purple things that had been splattered on the pavement and had stained it. The tree was full of these purple and bluish looking berries. They resembled small grapes. She picked a few from the tree and gave them to me to eat. I saw her put a few in her mouth, so I assumed they were good and decided to toss a few in my mouth as well. As soon as I did, the ripe sweetness melted in my mouth. It was like heaven on my tongue. I savored each bite. She told me they were "moras." Later I came to learn the English name for them — blackberries. To this day, I have not been able to find blackberries as sweet and juicy as those. Then again, it could have been the moment of peace and love that I was experiencing with my mom that made those blackberries taste so delicious. That sweet moment was one of several of that season of life, for we took the bus everywhere we went. That had been, and was now again, our bonding time.

Once my mother completed her year in rehab, she came to live with us. By that time, I was already well into fourth grade and was slowly making progress in school. I still struggled with reading and math, but my teachers were not giving up on me. With tutoring, my sister's help and my strong will to succeed, I was doing well. I knew though that while I was making progress in school, I was still behind everyone else. I also knew that I was not going to stay that way. I had made up my mind to make sure I succeeded and caught up. I worked very hard. I read every day. I paid attention in class and asked questions. I asked my friends for help when I needed it. I also worked to make new friends.

I had one best friend in particular, Adriana. Her mom would often call my mom to go over to clean her house. They became friends, and Adriana and I would go to each other's house. At school we both joined the cheerleading team. We were always in the back rows together because we were tall. We were taller than most girls our age. Adriana was the sociable and daring one. I was quiet and reserved — I was the one who was afraid to take risks. Our friendship was perfect because we balanced each other out. She would bring the boys over to talk, and I would remind her we were going to get into trouble. Most times one of her two brothers would come looking for us. It was fun being in fourth grade. That was the year I got "married" for the first time.

One day, I found out that a boy liked me, so my classmates decided we would get married. I did not want to, but they bugged me about it so much and promised we would get divorced before the end of the school day. Once they explained divorce, I succumbed to the pressure. "Oh, okay, I will marry him." They made rings out of paper for us and someone said something along the lines of, "You're married." I knew they would be expecting us to kiss, but I was not into boys yet, and although he was a little cute, it sure was not enough to entice me to kiss him. I think he was a little sad when I said, "I am not kissing you — that's so gross." He hung around me the rest of the day and that was very annoying. They did not tell me that being married meant someone would follow me all day long. As soon as the bell rang, I took off the ring and felt super free. I was divorced. We didn't remarry and he never hung around with me again. I was super busy, studying, learning how to make friends, and cheerleading.

My mother graduated from the rehab center and regained custody of Veronica and me. This new life was amazing. My mother decided to rent a smaller apartment in the same complex we lived in for her, my middle sister and me. She felt that I needed to remain in the same neighborhood and stay in the same school for stability. So we moved into the smaller place where the rent was cheaper. My older sister stayed in the apartment she was in with her boyfriend. It was nice because we all lived close together.

We lived in a studio the size of a small garage and my older sister lived in her two-bedroom apartment with her boyfriend. Since our studio apartment was small, all we could fit was a bunk bed for Veronica and me and a sofa bed for my mother. There was a counter with a sink and an electric stove for cooking in the same space. The whole area was taken up by the beds, the counter and our refrigerator. We also had a small TV. The bathroom was extremely narrow and small. We did not have a kitchen or a formal living room. I did not mind because it was a happy home — no more fighting and no more sleepless nights.

I often wondered about my stepfather. I felt a sense of sadness for him and gratitude at the same time. I had not heard from him or about him since I was taken to the foster home. My mother did not talk about him, and I did not ask. During that time, my mother began dating the friend who had helped her look for my older sister when she was kidnapped. His name was Henry and my mom had met him at work. He owned the carpet factory my mother worked in, so he was comfortable financially. He owned a home near Universal Studios, on one of the hills. When we would visit, I would run to the back yard and onto the hill that overlooked the freeway. It was fun to watch the cars speed by. Once in a while I would catch a glimpse of a deer or a skunk roaming the area. When I was not on the hill, I was swimming in his swimming pool. I loved that pool. I would spend hours swimming, pretending I was a mermaid. I pretended that I had a new magical place: The ocean. Since I no longer needed the forest to escape, I created another fun place to go to. The forest brought back memories that I was working so hard to forget. The ocean was my new place, full of peace and fun.

Henry was a lovely, generous man. He would often take us out to eat at fancy restaurants. He had a chauffeur and all he would say was, "Get the Mercedes ready, we are going out." We would all hop into his fancy car. I did not like the car much, as fancy as it was, because the interior upholstery was leather. It not only made me sweat during summer, but during winter, the leather was super cold. The smell of leather also gave me headaches, so I would be nauseated by each trip to wherever it was we were going.

I guess that's where I learned that the finer things were not always the best for me. My first experience at a fancy restaurant was a disaster. Going out to dinner were the only times we would get to dress up all fancy. I did not like dresses but once in a while I did not mind. The chauffeur drove us there and when we were seated, I almost had a panic attack. There were so many forks, spoons, cups and dishes. A small fork, a longer fork, and a really, really long fork. A small spoon, a bigger spoon, and an even bigger spoon. And let's not even talk about the dishes. There were plates on top of plates. What in the world was that all about? All I could think of was to try to watch other people and see what they did with them because I was not about to watch my mother. The only "fancy" place she would take me to was McDonald's. I also did not want to watch Henry because I figured he would think I was being weird. I needed to act as if I knew what to do, so I sat up straight on my chair, my hands crossed, and waited for our food. When they brought out the salad, I took a deep breath and grabbed the smallest fork. I looked at this beautiful salad. The presentation was gorgeous. I had never seen a salad so beautiful. The lettuce a deep green, not the regular lettuce I was used to. The red ripe tomatoes finely chopped, cheese and some other stuff I don't remember. I took my fork and gently stabbed some of the lettuce. My forked slipped on the plate and salad went flying everywhere. I was very embarrassed. My mother and Henry laughed and they slowly picked up the lettuce and tomatoes off the table and the floor. I gave up trying to be prim and proper and just ate the rest of my meal the way I always did.

That year was a happy year. I enjoyed fourth grade, my family was doing well and I continued making good progress at school. Then fifth grade rolled around and my life took another twist. My older sister and her boyfriend broke up and she moved in the studio with us. Now there were four of us in a studio the size of a garage. Nonetheless, I loved it. I loved having all of them there. We had all been looking forward to my mother marrying Henry. He was a kind man and had helped us a lot. Aside from taking us to places, he had given my mom a car and a microwave (we had never had a microwave). He had bought all of us expensive watches, and had given my mom what looked like an engagement ring. But that year, he died. I think he had a heart attack. My mother said he had developed diabetes from years of being a workaholic, skipping meals, and not eating healthy. The diabetes led to other illnesses and that finally took his life.

Chapter 12

The School Bully

We ended up having to move from the small studio apartment and into a bigger one because we were crowded. That same year I encountered a really mean bully. The "school bully." The kind of bully they make movies about. I don't remember the bully's name, but I remember she was a sixth grader. Not just any sixth grader, but the toughest, tallest and meanest one. She was not very girly. She never wore dresses and never properly combed her light blonde hair. It always looked like a beehive, all tangled up. She did not wear the nicest clothes either but that did not stop her from being popular. I think the only reason she was popular was because all the kids were afraid of her. She had an older sister who was in the seventh grade. She looked even taller and meaner. They were very scary and nobody wanted to mess with them. Every day after school her older sister would come over to our elementary school and instruct her little sister to go home right after school.

"Go home now, because I am fighting so and so" she'd say. Those were her exact words. I knew the words by heart because she would repeat them to her little sister every day. And sure enough somewhere behind some alley there was a fight and the next day we would all find out what we already knew to be true. The older sister would beat the living daylights out of whoever she fought.

The school bully and her sister had lots of fake friends, problem was I was not one of them. She intimidated me to the point that I did not want to be around her. Her bad energy made me want to stay as far away as possible. I must have been giving off some light or something because she would spot me wherever I was. I was a magnet for bullies. I figured that bullies are attracted to kids who are meek. Kids who are afraid and won't stand up for themselves. Kids with low self-esteem.

As much as I had been working on my self-esteem by doing better in school and joining cheerleading, I was not quite at courage yet. That's why she picked on me. I showed fear. It's like when dogs smell fear in a person, they will attack. The sixth grade bully was always ready to attack me. At least once a day she picked on me. She would do things like pass by me while I was eating lunch and punch me on the arm. It was not a light punch either. One time she left a bruise. We would all laugh, including me, but at the bottom of my heart I was embarrassed, scared and upset. She would make rude comments about me, in front of other kids as well.

Of all the emotions one feels when they are being bullied, the disappointment was the worst one for me to deal with. I was disappointed in myself. I was disappointed that I had many chances to tell someone, to tell a trusted adult, and I didn't. I had many chances to stand up for myself and say something. I did not because I did not want her to hate me more. I did not want to be a snitch. In the process I was hating myself. I was losing my self-esteem rapidly, and I was not happy. I wish I could have stood up for myself. I wish I asked her to leave me alone. But I did not want to ruffle anyone's feathers. I guess I wanted the comfortable feeling of things staying the same. But staying the same meant I was miserable. If I could turn back the clock, I would choose COURAGE!

My fifth grade year was about survival. I changed my school routine. I did not join cheer that year because all I wanted to do was to go home after school. I did not want to take the chance of being around her if I did not have to. I did however continue to make amazing improvement in reading and math. I was no longer being tutored and I could read as fast as the other kids. I was completing homework and spending time with my mother who had just bought a car and learned to drive.

That was the year I too began to learn to drive. My mother had been given a small old car, a two-door sedan. It was a red wine color and had no air conditioner. The radio had a spot for an A track, a big huge cassette. My mother and my sister would let me pull the car into the driveway. They would also let me move it forward and back. That was the closest to driving I got, and I loved it. Things were going great for me at home. My best friend Adriana and I became even closer. Her mom and my mom were spending more time together. Although she came from a two-parent home, her dad was never really around. My older sister moved out to another home that year, and so did we. Adriana's mom rented us her converted garage in the back of her home. It was a little bigger than the studio we lived in. It was bright and comfortable. Adriana and I would go shopping together and we would have slumber parties at her house. We would often spend hours in the backyard creating dance routines to some of our favorite songs. Living so close to her was fun.

Sixth grade, my final year in elementary school, was much better. The school bully had moved on to junior high school so I did not see her often. She would sometimes come after school following in her big sister's footsteps. She would come to tell some of the sixth graders that she would be getting into a fight in the popular alley by the liquor store. I stayed as far away as I could when I saw her all pumped up and ready to fight. I did not understand why she would feel the need to want to fight all the time. It seemed like a very sad life. She must have had so much anger from living in a bad home, or maybe bad things happened to her that she felt that the only way to deal with it was to beat up other kids. Kids who for whatever stupid reason she did not like. Although I did not understand it then, I still felt sorry for her. Living that way seemed like it was only going to eventually lead her into one place: Jail.

Adriana and I had the same teacher, Mr. Duggan. All I remember is that he was a cool teacher and we always had fun in his classroom. That year we bought our yearbooks, bought our clothes for graduation and went to science camp. Science camp was the best. That was only the second time I had been away from my family, but this time it was for a good reason. The first time was when I was in the foster home. I remember the girls having their own cabins and the boys on the other side of the campground in theirs. We had day hikes and night hikes and in one of those night hikes I ended up being the talk of the campground. While crossing a small creek I lost my footing and fell into it. I was soaked and muddy. Everyone laughed. I laughed too. My laugh was genuine because it was truly funny. I was happy that I had given them a funny memory and an opportunity to tell a great story. I was of course the center of attention so I could not complain. That's when I first learned that laughing at myself was the best thing ever. I have not stopped since.

One night the boys came into our cabins while we were out hiking. We came back to see underwear, bras and shirts hanging on trees. That was done without their supervisor's permission, so they got into trouble. But it was hilarious. Thank goodness they did not have a chance to go through my stuff. After coming back from camp we created a memory book and my fall into the creek made it to the number one spot of the funniest moments of our trip. I would be remembered forever.

The day of our sixth grade graduation came. I wore a pink fitted dress with a small vest, my dark brown hair curled to perfection. My sister helped me get ready for it as she had helped me get ready for other special events. For this event, thank goodness, she kept me rated G. She was usually in charge of choosing my Halloween outfits. To keep it simple she would just make an extra costume of exactly what she would wear to go out to a nightclub. Mind you my sister was twenty-two years old and she loved to party. I always looked up to her and thought she was gorgeous. She looked different from me though. Not as tall and her skin was a milky white, mine was more of a pale yellow. She had light blonde hair and her makeup was always done beautifully. She always wore really nice clothes and she looked very attractive in them. She kept her body in shape. I admired everything about her, and wanted to be like her. So I trusted her judgment in costumes for Halloween.

I am not sure how I was never sent home on Halloween looking the way I did. One year I was a cave woman and the dress I wore was about half an inch below my butt. If I bent down, my underwear would have shown. Not to mention that it was fitted very tightly to my body. Thank goodness I did not have curves yet otherwise suspension would have been appropriate. She also did my hair and makeup and it was amazing. I had thick black eyeliner that made my eyes look big and bold and dark eye shadow to add a touch of daring. She would apply really dark mascara to enhance the effects of making my eyes stand out. I wore bright red lipstick and my hair was teased to the point that I looked like the Lion King. Add some nude sandals and I looked eighteen but without the curves. Another Halloween she was a bunny. Not just a regular bunny but a sexy bunny. So of course, I was a bunny too, just not as pretty as her. The outfit I wore was not quite appropriate for school. It was a pink bathing suit (very fitted) with white leotards and high heels. And then there's the dark eyeliner, dark eyeshadow and red lipstick. Bunny ears and bunny tail included. I don't know how I got away with it. And yes, that's how I would go trick or treating.

Graduation day was different — no inappropriate attire and no heavy makeup. I did wear nylons and high heels. I felt comfortable and beautiful, sitting amongst my fellow students, excitedly waiting to hear my name called for my diploma. Many thoughts came rushing. I was in awe that I had survived twelve years of such hardship. I could not believe that my life consisted of so many obstacles that I was able to overcome. Memories of my sisters being beaten, my mother being dragged by the car, the fights, the gun, the many nights I had spent in the closet. I thought of my animals, my stepfather of whom we had not heard about anymore, my sleepless nights on the floor next to my mother passed out, all the quarters I had dug into the dirt for God to have, and my imaginary place in the forest that I no longer visited. I thought about the day that changed my life forever. The events that had brought me to this place, to this day. I thought about the lady from the state that had taken me away from my family. I wondered if she thought about me and how I was doing. Did she remember me still? She would have been happy to see that her taking me away was one of the best things that have ever happened to me. Even though I did not know this lady, her one act of taking me from my home, of going with her gut feeling that something was wrong had saved me. Had saved all of us.

"Elva Alicia Leon." Over the loudspeakers, my name was called and my train of thought was broken. I stood up quickly and began walking toward the stage, all the while trying my best not to fall or slip with the high heels I was wearing. I walked up to accept my diploma, shook the principal's hand and looked around in the crowd searching for my family, my mom and my sisters. A thought crossed my mind. Four years ago my teachers would have bet I would have never made it past each grade without being held back. Not only had I never been held back in school, but I was one of the students with the highest GPA receiving my diploma that year.

I accepted my diploma and walked back to my seat. I could see my older sisters and my mom cheering for me. My heart filled with such love and pride. To make them proud was the greatest feeling ever. That was when the thought that I would attend college was solidified. College had never been considered before. The word seemed foreign to me. Going to college was not discussed in elementary school, unfortunately. But thank goodness for my older sister who always had perfect timing for everything. She gave me a hug and congratulated me after the ceremony, looked me in the eyes and in her usual strong and confident voice, she said, "You are going to college." Her words changed the course of my life. It seemed like she knew that that was where my life needed to go even before I did. "College — yup, I'm going to college." Up until that point, all I knew about college was that it was another kind of school we would go to and it was important. I did not know how I would get there, but I knew it was special, and I was going.

That was a huge step in believing in myself and in preparing to take control of my own destiny. I made a statement, and I was going to stick with it no matter what. "I am going to college!"

Chapter 13

Nightmares and Dreams

That summer my mother rekindled her relationship with my stepfather. He asked that we move back in with him — back to our old house. The house where all those bad things had happened; the house from where I had been removed. The last time I was there was when I was nine years old and the social worker took me to pack my belongings and say good-bye to my mother.

My mother thought it would be a good idea to move back but she consulted me first and asked my thoughts about it. I loved my stepfather even though I did not have a very close bond with him. I knew he had our best interest at heart and would do anything to make sure we were safe. So moving back seemed like a good idea. It became a great idea after thinking about the fact that if we stayed, I would end up at the same junior high as the bully, who would be an eighth grader and I a seventh grader. I had had to deal with her in fifth grade and I couldn't bear the thought of having to deal with her in the seventh grade. My whole life flashed before my eyes at that moment and saw myself being beaten up on a daily basis by this bully. I did not hesitate to tell my mother, "Let's move." That summer we packed our TV, the bunk beds, my mother's bed, a small refrigerator, our clothes, and we left East Los Angeles to return to El Monte.

All was well in our home after we moved back, until shortly after I began to have awful nightmares again. I had a few early on in my childhood but now they were getting worse. Sleeping by myself was very difficult as the panic and fear would set in right before I began getting ready for bed. When my sister was not home and sleeping next to me on the extra bed, I would ask my mother to take her place. So, I never really slept alone. I suffered from panic attacks as well. I was scared of the dark and would often feel things around me. I would feel them mostly at night when all was quiet. When I fell asleep my nightmares would wake me up, and I would crawl into bed with my mom. She was either sleeping in my room and if she was in hers, I would run to her bed. She had a bed in the laundry room, next to the washer and dryer. I never really saw her and my stepfather share a room.

My nightmares were always the same. It was some dark energy holding me hostage in my room. The room I was in was not lit. I would try to run out but the doors and windows would suddenly shut and I was unable to get out. I could not fully explain, but it was a feeling of invisible hands, many of them holding me back. I could not run or scream and an immense fear would overcome me. I would wake up paralyzed from the fear. My eyes would be open but my body would not allow me to move. I had to force myself to scream or at least move a finger. Eventually, all my body would wake up. I had to sleep with lights or the TV on. I would often stay up late because I did not want to go to sleep. I knew that if I fell asleep I would have nightmares again. Always the same nightmare. I held on to being awake for as long as I could and eventually the exhaustion from sleep deprivation would conquer my fear and I would fall asleep. Nightmare to follow.

I enrolled at Kranz Junior High and was really excited about my new middle school. The school was directly behind my house with only a metal fence separating the large field and my backyard. My stepfather no longer had the animals. The city had outlawed animals in that zone, so my stepfather had to sell all of them with the exception of the chickens and dogs. The school was nice. I could use the alley that was next to my house to walk there but I was too lazy, and my mother would drive me to school. I would hop in the car and she would drive me to the front of the school. I was there in a minute. I had good classes there. I had typing, which I excelled in, and wood shop, which was super fun. I had reading, writing, math and science. Every day my mom would drive me to school and she would rush back from her housekeeping job in Santa Monica to pick me up from school. She would make me dinner and often make me lunch when she did not have to go to work. She would pass plates with *carne asada* (a marinated cooked meat), rice and beans over the fence for me and a few friends that I had made. They loved my mother's cooking. After school I would come home, eat dinner, lock myself in my room and do homework. I spent hours doing homework and making sure it was perfect.

I gave it my all when it came to school. I had put so much effort into making sure I did well at school that one month I became Student of the Month. In the entire school, once a month, they would choose one student to be Student of the Month, another student for Most Improved and another for Citizenship. The principal would choose the students who excelled in those areas. That particular month I was part of that group. I could not believe it. My hard work and the fact that the teachers had not given up on me had paid off. "If they could only see me now," I thought. I went from the dumbest student to the smartest one. I remember going home and giving my mom the good news. She was so proud of me. She told me that for every "A" that I earned at school, she would give me twenty dollars. I made quite some money that first trimester. Even though the money was nice to have, I would have earned "A's" whether she paid me or not. The feeling of accomplishment far exceeded the fact that I had money in my pocket. That feeling was the one that made me work so hard. It was seeing those A's and feeling so proud of myself that gave me the dedication to continue working.

The day I received my Student of the Month Award was a special one. The school held an entire assembly just for the two of us. Our names were also displayed on the school marquee. I made my mom take dozens of pictures of the marquee and of my award. It was the second recognition I had received for my hard work, the first being my diploma. The taste of victory and accomplishment was one I savored for a long time. I made it my mission to try to win as many awards as possible. During those two years at Kranz, I excelled. What I could not get over was the fact that I was an introvert. I was still shy and being taller than the rest of my classmates did not help. I was also harboring a deep dark secret. Something I was too embarrassed to talk about. A secret that haunted me for many years — my nightmares.

I began having nightmares around the age of seven. I was in middle school and not only had they come back but they became worse. I remember being seven and my nightmares starting off as confusing dreams. In my dreams I would visit places that during my waking moments I had never been to. I would see people whom I had never met before, but in my dreams, it was as if I knew them very well. These dreams were a bit scary, but the ones that were truly torturous to me were the dreams where I felt trapped. The nightmare would always begin the same way. I would be in my home alone, in El Monte, where the fights had occurred. I would either be in my room or in the living room when all of a sudden the doors and windows would close. Everything around me was gloomy and dark — an omniscient gray. As soon as the doors and windows would shut, my heart would begin to race and blood-curdling fear would set in. I would panic and would want to leave. I wanted to bolt out of the house and out the door, but a force would hold me back. It was as if I was trying to walk and hurricane winds were holding me back, but instead of winds, they were like hands. Invisible hands pulling me back. Lots and lots of hands.

I feared dying that way — being held back by an unseen force; being murdered by something I could not see. Ghosts. Oftentimes I would hear my name being called while I was trying to escape. It was a voice that came from nowhere and everywhere at the same time. In my dream I fought hard to escape. I would scream and kick all the while feeling like my feet were trapped in thick mud. Unable to walk, unable to move, the immense fear and the sense of screaming would wake me. I would wake up with my heart pounding, like it was beating a thousand beats a second and about to burst. I would wake up with the same immense fear I felt in my dream, unable to catch my breath, too scared to move. I was scared that even when awake, that unseen force would pull me back. Slowly I would stand up, take a few small steps toward the door, preparing for the forces to pull me back. I would run to the nearest room hoping to find my mother so that I could sleep with her. I remember asking my mother many times not to fall asleep until I had fallen asleep. She would ask what the matter was and I would simply respond with, "I am scared." I never told her of what. I would check her eyes to make sure she was still awake, if she was I would close mine, and then I would quickly open them up to double check that she was still awake.

My sister would often say that the reason I was scared was because of all the scary movies I would watch. For a while I did watch a lot of scary movies.

I was into the Nightmare on Elm Street movies. I watched all of them. The premise: a killer dressed in black, tattered pants and a red and white stripped sweater, his face deformed from severe burns and one of his hands was a glove made with knives for each finger. He would kill people in their dreams. So maybe, just maybe, my sister could be right. Too many scary movies when I was young. I had stopped watching those but my nightmares did not stop. I was in eighth grade when I had one of the worst nightmares.

It began as a usual deep falling into nothingness. I opened my eyes in my dream and was back in my living room. Nobody was there. Immediately the fear set in. Right at that moment I knew where this was headed, so I wanted to run out the front door as quickly as possible before the doors and windows began to shut on me. Before I could take the first steps, they began to shut quickly. I tried to run to open the door, but I could not. When I turned around, I saw it. For the first time I was able to see what was holding me back. There were at least fifteen to twenty clouds of smoke behind me, all in their own separate space. That was what was holding me back. Again, my name would be called. It was a soft voice and would say my name over and over again. "Alicia." Nothing else. I tried to scream as loud as I could, but to no avail. I screamed again. I knew I was having a nightmare and I needed to scream to snap myself out of it. This time I managed to scream loud enough to wake myself up. My eyes were open, but my body could not move. I could not scream, cry or lift my hand, but I could see everything in my room. I could hear the noise in the kitchen. I was caught between a dream state and an awake state.

At that time the internet didn't exist so I was not able to google what had just happened to me. It was not until I was in my early thirties that I learned about this. Sleep paralysis they call it. So at the time I kept the theory that something was trying to possess me. I'm pretty sure all those scary movies did not help. Try going to sleep on that thought every night. For the next few years, the lights or the TV was on all night. Sometimes, I would bring my cat or dog inside to sleep with me when neither my mom nor sister felt the need to go to bed early. It did not help the nightmares, but it made it easier to fall asleep knowing another soul was with me and would be there when I woke up. I learned to deal with my nightmares somewhat, but many times I would go to school half asleep because I would stay awake at night too afraid to sleep and too embarrassed to wake my mother up. After a while, my mother decided she needed her own room. By then, both of my sisters had already moved out.

I went through my two junior high school years living with my nightmares but also giving my all in school. I was an honor student and well on my way to accomplish many things. College for one. My older sister always instilled in me that I would go to college. She made me believe in myself and never questioned the fact that I would. That was what I worked for. I had my dreams. I had my plans. I would go to a university somewhere in another state. I wanted to experience being out in the world alone. Somewhere far away. I was not quite sure where, I just knew it would be far. I wanted to see new people and taste different foods. I wanted to see new landmarks and have fun adventures. By this time, my middle school had given us many talks about going to college. They gave us tons of information, so I was well versed on what college entailed. I graduated from junior high school and entered high school. That was a huge deal. Being in high school felt more like being an adult versus the young kid in junior high.

I attended Mountain View High School. It was a little further from my house, but I did not mind the distance. Walking there would take me about a half an hour, but my mother would drive me there. As a ninth grader, I was at the bottom of the totem pole, just like most of the ninth graders. There were exceptions, the outgoing ninth graders. They were at the top of the lower part of the totem pole. Meaning, they could blend in with sophomores because they were a little more popular. The bottom of the totem pole had to steer clear from sophomores, juniors and especially seniors. As freshmen the last thing we wanted was attention. Neither good nor bad. For me, that was important. I was never good with attention. I did not have many friends and socializing gave me anxiety. Adriana had been my only long lasting friend and now we were miles apart. The girls in my junior high were just friends I happened to hang out with during nutrition and lunch. They were not friends I could confide my problems or worries to. The beautiful thing about it was that I was completely and utterly okay with it.

I did end up joining a group of students I called the smart group. They were always in the library or just relaxing and talking about school. It was easier to be around them because they focused on school instead of teenage issues like who's dating who or who liked who. We would talk about our classes and our grades. Many times we would have reading competitions. A girl in the group who eventually became my friend, Claudia, and I would compete to see who could read more chapter books on a given day. I don't remember who would win, but it made reading more exciting. I read many V.C. Andrews novels. The first novel was about children who were locked up in a basement and neglected by their mother. The love of reading carried me through to my adult years.

Chapter 14
Mirror, Mirror on the Wall

It was during my freshman year that I began to blossom and boys began to look a little more interesting. Up until then, boys had never been a thought for me. It was a surprise to me when I developed a crush on a senior that year. Don't ask me his name because sadly I don't remember. All I know is that he was one of the more popular seniors. I do remember that he was tall and had a nice build. His smile was what I remember the most. I loved his smile because it gave an impression that he was a cool down to earth kind of guy. Any chance I had, I would stare at him. Usually during nutrition or lunch. Sometimes I would get lucky enough to see him while I was taking papers to the office. I wouldn't stare in a creepy way, or where it was really obvious, but just enough to glance and fantasize that he was my boyfriend. I went as far as buying a picture with him in it during a picture sale once.

The school took many pictures of the seniors at the dances and sold them for one dollar during nutrition. I remember browsing through the pictures for sale just to kill time and, to my surprise, I found one with him and three of his friends in it. It looked like it might have been taken during the Homecoming Dance because he was dressed in a black suit and had a striped tie to go with it. He looked rather handsome. I thought long and hard about buying the picture. I felt kind of creepy buying a picture of someone who did not know I existed. Having a crush on him was one thing, but buying a picture and him not knowing I had it, was too stalker-ish. After much thought I paid the dollar and was given the picture to take home in a small, brown paper bag. I felt a little embarrassed that the student I had paid the dollar to knew that I had bought a picture that I was not even in. "Would she think weird of me?" I ignored the feeling and went on to my next class. I held onto that picture for a long time. I would often take it out and look at it and pretend he had given it to me. I laugh at the silliness now, but at the time it was serious stuff.

Things changed toward the end of my freshman year. I became more sociable. I was invited to my first slumber party and I had mixed emotions about it. Usually I tried to stay away from doing anything with friends after school because I did not want to connect with them emotionally. I figured that if I got attached to anyone, losing them as a friend would surely hurt, and I just could not deal with that kind of pain. I had experienced it when I no longer had Adriana as my best friend. So after school, my routine had been the same. I would eat a snack, do homework, eat dinner, dance in my room for exercise for a while and then take a shower and go to sleep. Nothing too exciting.

So here I was, with a slumber party invitation in my hand, in awe of how this had happened. All of my life I had lived trying to stay hidden from the world. Kids stayed away from me and I stayed away from them. This was the day I crossed the boundaries of a loner to considering myself somewhat sociable. I had made a few friends, mostly bookworm friends. Girls who enjoyed school like I did. Making friends with them was easy. We did not have to talk about our personal lives to have fun. Gossip was not important to us, nor were boys for that matter. We focused on academics — books and reading and our classes were what we discussed.

I looked at the invitation long and hard and decided it was time to join the real world. I decided I would go. My mother was already a few years sober. She had not taken any alcohol in a long while nor had she and my stepfather fought. Everything was going well. I remember asking her for permission and she quickly said yes to my request. I don't know why she said yes, so quickly. It could have been her guilt, the guilt she carried about me going into a foster home, or maybe she was just being nice. It did not matter.

My mother drove me to the house where the party would be. She wanted to know where I was going and who I would be with. It was kind of weird, her being worried about me and all. I arrived and all the girls were there in their pajamas eating. They seemed really excited to see me arrive, which made me feel welcomed. It felt like I belonged there. I set my bag of clothes down and quickly joined them. We ate and played games. The most popular game we played was the one where we would try not to fall asleep. The people who would fall asleep would have their face painted or we would put some kind of condiment like ketchup or mustard on their hair. I helped paint a few faces and hung a couple of underwear from hangers on the wall. It was a lot of fun. I was spared from all the pranks being pulled because I was one of the last ones to fall asleep.

The beginning of my sophomore year was a bit more challenging. That was the year I had my first boyfriend. Jesse came to my house without me knowing him. He was a twelfth grader (a senior) and I was a sophomore. The story he tells is that he had seen me around the school and he developed a crush on me. Apparently, I had seen him once, when the volleyball I was practicing at school with rolled away from our team and I had to go retrieve it. Jesse came across the ball and handed it to me.

When he told me that story, I vaguely remembered the incident. I guess he did not make a huge impression because I remembered the incident but not him. He came over my house once, when I was not home, introduced himself to my mother and asked if he could take me out. My mother thought he was a nice kid. He had arrived from Mexico some years ago to live with his older brother, so his Spanish was very fluent. That might have impressed my mother. When I got home my mother told me about his visit. I had no clue of who he could be. I insisted to my mother that I was not ready to go out with boys. She, however, felt that I needed to socialize a little more. To her, doing homework and staying in my room did not seem healthy. She would later tell me she came to regret pushing me to go out with Jesse.

Our first date was far from romantic. It was a teenage date. We went to McDonald's for dinner. We sat and talked. I don't remember the conversation because it was probably about school or something. He bought me food and wrote something nice on a napkin. I kept that napkin for many years. That date turned into another and another. I guess we had things in common and enjoyed each other's company. We began to spend time with each other. It got to the point where I began to neglect my friends and the social events that took place at school to spend time with him.

Now I look back and wish I could have balanced my time. I missed out on many fun things at school to sit on the grass with my boyfriend. I missed out on spending time with friends and talking about college or silly things to spend time with someone I was not going to be with forever. I can't take those days back much as I would like to. Once high school days are gone, well they are gone. So there are some regrets in my life.

Our relationship began to deepen and spending time with Jesse became more important than anything else, including school. I began to neglect my school work. My grades began to drop and my teachers asked me why. I did not have an answer. My mother allowed us to use her car and she would sometimes even give us money. She trusted me because I had been responsible in school that she figured I would be responsible in making choices as well.

She was wrong. I did not know the first thing about having a boyfriend. All the freedom she gave me was way too much. Looking back, she should have monitored my freedom a little more closely; she should have asked more questions, talked to me about growing up and being responsible. She was not aware that my grades were dropping.

By this time, I had my driver's permit, so I would take my mother's car to school. Jesse and I would use it to get to school, go out for lunch and to hang out after school. Jesse had mentioned that his ex-girlfriend was not happy with his choice of new girlfriend — me. I did not think anything of it until she and her friends (seven of them) began to follow me during the switching of classes. They would stare, make comments, and then laugh. I felt uneasy but I did not think much of it since it came with the territory. I figured that she still had feelings for him and would get over them soon. Anyway, those girls were kind of scary. They were seniors, but they were not ordinary seniors. These were the "mean girls" of the school and they had muscles and looked like men. They were really big. They participated in every sport (I think they lifted weights).

Things with the girls began to get worse. Other kids began to come up to me and tell me that they were planning something evil. I figured maybe they would just come up to me and we would clear this up. But that's not what happened.

After coming back from eating lunch at Tommy's one afternoon, Jesse and I noticed a group of people hanging out in the parking lot. This was unusual as everyone who parked their car in the school parking lot would usually enter the school grounds immediately. We parked and got off the car. As we began heading towards the classroom, we saw it was the "mean girls." Yup, all seven of them. Walking as a bunch, they looked like one of those bulldozers. Seriously, it was frightening. Before I could think about what could possibly happen, the girls were within inches of me. Jesse stepped in between me and them. Then "BAM" I was grabbed by my hair by someone behind me. I was so focused on his ex in front of me that I did not see one of her friends make her way behind me. She grabbed me by my hair and pulled me to the floor. I fell on my back and the impact of my head hitting the ground caused me to black out for a few seconds. When I regained consciousness, I saw his ex-girlfriend, Rosa, on top of me scratching and punching my face. I did not feel any pain. It was as if my body had shut down any feeling and I was just an observer, watching this young girl tear at my face with her nails. As I looked behind her I saw Jesse on top of her trying to get her off, and on top of him girls trying to get him off of her. It was like a bad dream where I was paralyzed, unable to escape. Next thing I know Rosa was being pulled off me by a teacher who had made it in time to spare me a few more blows. Still struggling to figure out what was happening, I gained a few moments of clarity and decided to defend myself. As I was lying on the floor my reaction to instinctively kick came. However, she was too far by this time and my kick was in vain. The teacher helped me up and I began to make sense of what had just happened.

As I walked toward the office, my body began to shake uncontrollably. I still did not feel any pain, but I began to feel ashamed. Embarrassed. A crowd of students watched my walk of shame, staring at me. I did not know it at the time, but the look on their faces did not seem right. They saw something I couldn't. What was it? I would not find out until I reached the office.

When I entered the office, I was asked to sit and wait for the principal. I seemed lost. I still had not fully understood what had happened to me. The school office called my mom, and she and my sister came right down. I still hadn't seen the damage. All I could do was sit in that office and shake.

When my sister and mother entered the office, the look of horror on their faces scared me. As soon as they saw me, they began to cry. They had the same facial expressions that the kids had as I walked to the office. I felt bad to see them cry. I think my heart broke more for the pain I had caused them than for what had happened to me. Until I saw my face that is.

My sister asked me to wash my face in the bathroom. I walked over to use the nurse's bathroom. I went in and locked the door behind me. I turned around and saw the mirror. I could not believe my eyes. It took me a while to digest what I was looking at. I had vertical red marks running down my entire face. Red swollen marks. She had scratched my entire face. I realized why the horror in everyone's faces. I realized why my mother and older sister were crying. They could not bear to see my swollen scratched up face. Neither could I.

I stood there looking at myself in the mirror for a few seconds until my legs gave in, and I had to sit down on the cold bathroom floor in a fetal position. I bawled as I covered my face with both hands. She had scratched my face and scarred me for life. I knew it. Her aim was to scar my face for life. My heart broke. I did not deserve it. Why did she want to hurt me that way? I had never done anything to her. I did not care who she was or what she did. I hardly ever mentioned her name. She was not important to me. I guess I was to her.

Sitting there sobbing on that cold, empty bathroom floor, I had to compose myself. I had to do it for the sake of my sister and my mother. I washed my face without looking at myself in the mirror again. I walked outside with my head held high. Taking another look at me, my mother began to cry again. Finally, she said "Don't worry, we will put some aloe Vera on your scars." I was suspended from school for a week, along with Jesse and the other girls.

My mother drove the car home without a word. When we reached home, she applied aloe Vera on my face. In the Mexican culture, aloe Vera is used to help strengthen skin and to remove scarring. As she placed the fresh aloe she had cut from the yard, my thoughts began to run. Rosa had been planning this for days. She wanted to ruin my face. She had done it.

Jesse called that night and apologized. After four months or so of dating, he had been good to me. The next day after the fight, I got up to go to the bathroom. I was scared to see myself in the mirror. I was still in denial about my face being scarred. Actually, I was still in shock about the whole incident. Until then I had never been in trouble at school. I had been a straight A student and I got along well with all my teachers. After much thought, I decided I wanted to see how the aloe had worked. Hesitantly, I stood in front of the mirror. It took me a few seconds to build up my courage to look at myself. I held my head down until I was ready. I lifted my head and looked at myself in the mirror. To my amazement I realized that a miracle had occurred. I examined my swollen face and I found that the swelling had not come from my face being sliced by Rosa's fingernails, she had simply rubbed her fingernails over my skin. I could not understand how during the entire time she was scratching and tearing at my face not once did she cut through my skin. She had only superficially rubbed my skin. Unbelievable!

I stared at my face for a long time. I tried to comprehend how her nails had not cut through my skin. I know a few times I've scratched myself with my own nails that left a slight scar on my leg or arm. Her nails were long and sharp, yet she did not do any damage. My mother never talked about miracles, but somehow I knew this had to be one of them.

After my suspension, my mother, my sister and I went to school to meet with the principal and everyone else involved. The first thing I saw were the faces on the "mean girls" when they saw me. They were priceless. My face was back to its normal self. Not one sign of damage — flawless. I smiled as I went in. My sister and my mother went in and we all sat down. Soon after, my sister began to state her demands on my behalf. I loved the way my sister would fight battles for me. She would do it in such a confident and assertive manner. I admired her guts.

She demanded that Rosa stay away from me or else she would get the police involved. My counselor, who was also Rosa's counselor, favored Rosa. She had worked for him as a student aid so I was sure they had built a bond of some sort. After the meeting, Rosa would be in his office regularly and would smirk when she saw me. She would do it as if to say, "Ha, I am on good terms with the counselor."

As the saying goes, "The sweetest revenge is major success." After high school, I would come across Rosa working at a swap-meet, looking like a homeless person. I had no traces of scarring on my face and I was well on my way to success attending college. Revenge was sweet.

After the school fight, things began to go downhill for Jesse and me. I experienced the first episode of physical abuse. Abuse that would go on for seven years. The first incident happened four months into our relationship while we were sitting on the grassy field of the school behind my house. My mother could not see us, nor could we see her because we were a couple of houses away. We figured we needed some time alone. I remember it clearly. It's one of those moments that is seared in my memory, the feelings, the smell, the way the sunlight lit the whole campus as we sat in the cool shade of some trees.

I don't know how it started. I am sure it was some teenage nonsense. I remember it being an ordinary conversation that quickly turned ugly. I said something about another boy at the school; it was a joke. I had meant it to be a sarcastic remark, but he didn't take it well. I saw Jesse's face light up with anger. His eyes became wider and red and his face perked up. Within a second, I saw his hand swinging across and slapping my face. There was no pain at the time. I was more shocked and dazed than anything. Funny how the body works, when you don't expect pain it takes a minute to process what it felt like, a pretty long minute. I did not know whether to cry or not. I was not sure what to do, get up and leave or stay. But before the pain set in and before I could muster the courage to get up and leave, Jesse quickly hugged me and asked for forgiveness.

That was when the pain started setting in — the heat of his heavy hand on my cheek, the redness and swelling that was beginning to form. The pain was difficult to understand. Prior to this I had never experienced pain from someone hitting me. I had never been hit. I had seen my sisters get torturously beaten by my mother and I had seen my mother and stepfather physically attack each other. The most pain I felt from another human being was the attack by his ex-girlfriend and my hair being pulled by my mother.

The interesting thing was that for so long, I had wished that I would be beaten too. I would wish that my mother would include me in her unfair beatings of my sisters. I did not want to feel like I was betraying them or allowing them to take the wrath of my mother alone. I wanted to feel their pain; I wanted to know what it was like to be slapped and punched; I wanted to share in their sorrows. I wanted them to know that I loved them so much that I wanted to suffer too. But it never happened. Now I was experiencing the pain I had prayed for. Is this what my sisters felt? It took me a few minutes to process the apology from Jesse. "I am sorry I didn't mean it." I wasn't sure how to react. Part of me felt like it was a bad thing and another part of me felt that it was okay. A few minutes later we got up as Jesse felt it was important for me to put ice on my cheek. As we walked toward the house many thoughts raced through my head. I found it difficult to sort out my emotions. I figured it was a one-time incident and it would never happen again. I was wrong.

My sophomore year had come to a close. I did not sign up for summer school although I needed it badly. My grades had been suffering because of my relationship with Jesse and the amount of time I was spending with him. My grades had gone from straight A's in my honors courses to C's or D's. The way I dressed also changed. I no longer cared to dress nicely. Before Jesse, I would shop for clothes once a week. I would make sure my clothes matched and my hair was as nicely styled as could be. I would take time to put my curlers on at night and wake up in the morning to neat curls I could pin up. Now I would wear sweats and sweatshirts to school and my hair in a ponytail. I even wore sunglasses with my sweats and ponytail, not sure what I was thinking. I know now what was happening.

Jesse was slowly taking me away from what I knew was a strong foundation that would be the key to my future success. He decided that school was not in my best interest. Slowly, my friends were disappearing. I no longer had a bond with the few friends I had and I most definitely was not making any new ones. I did attend a dance or two with Jesse but for the most part, his insecurities made sure that I always stayed near him. Mingling with friends was not an option. I remember one of my teachers pulling me aside one day and asking if I was alright. "Elva, I noticed you have been wearing sweats to school and sunglasses, this is very unusual for you, is everything okay?" he asked. "Yes, everything is fine." I lied. I guess it was not a lie because at the time I truly believed everything was okay. I was losing my identity, I was losing the very grain of my being, my soul. I was also losing what I had worked so hard for — my education.

The rest of the summer I don't remember much. My memory jumps forward to registration time when I had to register for the following year's classes. I was sitting in the cafeteria next to about a hundred other students waiting their turn to get their classes. I went through all the steps and then like a car hitting a brick wall at 100 mph, I was jolted by the terrible information that this year, my junior year, I would not be allowed in honors courses. I could not believe it; no honors English, no honors Science and no honor's Social Studies. I would not be allowed in debate again, all of this due to the failing grades I had gotten during my sophomore year. I could not and would not accept this. There was absolutely no way I would register for regular classes. I was not regular. I had struggled so hard to get to this point. The point of being in honors courses, the point of letting my sisters know I was an advanced student and bringing home straight A's. And what was I going to tell my mother? How would I explain this to my older sister? She believed in me. She believed I would attend college. I feared letting my sister down more than I did my mother.

As I waited with my schedule of classes in my hand to be inputted into the computer by the counselor, I decided I had to do something. I could not allow this atrocity to happen. Luckily for me, my schedule had been written in pencil on a small sheet of paper. It was like my entire life depended on this little square piece of paper. I did what I knew was wrong. I erased the regular classes I had been signed up for and wrote myself in for the honor's classes. This was obviously illegal, and if I had been caught I would have been suspended.

At the time, everything was done by hand. There were no fast computers to send information quickly, no internet. There were only old computers. So we all had to stand in one line and then another and then another. It was difficult for someone to keep track of the shenanigans that were going on. My hand began to sweat as I erased one class after another and rewrote them. My heart was beating a thousand beats per minute from the fear that I would get caught. I was sure someone would see me. My forehead began to sweat and drops landed on the sheet of paper making some of it illegible. I walked up to the counselor who was ready to input my classes. He took one good look at me and then at my schedule. I believed he would know that I did not belong to those classes. It was over for me. But then, his fingers began typing on the keyboard and within a few minutes he notified me that I would get my schedule in the mail and wished me a good day.

I had gotten away with it. I could not believe how easy it had been, yet extremely afraid. I had to keep my place in line and erase and rewrite classes within a short amount of time. I felt horrible because I knew that I had not earned the right to take those classes. Those classes were for people who worked their behinds off, not slackers like me. I had not been willing to do the work. But I justified it in my mind. I rationalized that it was perfectly fine to do it. I would prove to the teachers that I was capable of keeping up. I had made one mistake and I had the right to be given a second chance even if it meant that I would give it myself. I knew, however, that life doesn't work that way. In the real world, if you make a mistake you have to pay the consequence; there are sometimes no second chances.

Walking home that day I had the worst feeling in my stomach. I felt ashamed and disappointed in myself. I had failed my classes and I had lied. That feeling was worse than if I had just dealt with the consequence of taking regular classes. Now that I think about it, I would have done well in them and then signed on for honors classes during my senior year. It is one of the moments in my life that I wish I could take back.

Chapter 15

The Darkest Day

That summer I spent most of my time with Jesse. My mother never set boundaries for me, nor did she ask questions about where I was going or where I was. I don't remember any abuse from Jesse during that time. I spent all my time with him and had no friends to cause friction between us. I did everything he said and therefore we did not have problems. Once school began in my junior year, it had turned badly. Jesse had already graduated and I had no one to spend my time with at school. All my friends had made new friends and it was difficult to join their groups. The library became my new best friend. I spent all of my nutrition and lunch recess in the library. It was pretty sad but I guess I had to pay for neglecting my friends the year before. I was not into my studies as much as I had been before. The classes I had registered myself into were beginning to take a toll on me because I could not keep up. Not doing well the year before had caused me to miss so much of my education and it affected me that year. Homework was no longer a priority so that set me back even more. I no longer planned to attend college. All I cared about was spending time with Jesse.

I guess the attention from a man was something that I wanted more than to think about my future. Maybe growing up without a father gave me the longing for a male figure in my life. Now that school has started, going out became an issue for my mother. She began to notice that I was no longer coming home to do homework. I was no longer receiving awards and report cards were nowhere in sight. One evening when I came home late, she asked where I had been. I gave her attitude and she snapped. She threw a shoe at me and nearly hit me in the face.

At that point I knew she was no longer going to be tolerant of what I was doing. She set rules that I was not to use the car anymore and that I was to come home right after school. Basically, I could not spend as much time with Jesse. As she said that, I snapped. So many thoughts raced through my head. He had been the only one left in my life; my friends were gone and my sisters were gone. I no longer had the pride in school I had before, nor the motivation to do better. And now she wanted to take the last thing I had. The only person who truly cared about me, who gave me all the attention I needed and made me feel special would no longer be there for me all the time.

Everything came crashing down on me, and by everything I mean all my past and present. All the emotions I had not dealt with — from the alcoholism, the abuse I saw in my home, the foster home I had been to, the courtroom, my sisters, my mom, my stepfather, my grades going down, losing my friends, lying to get classes, and now Jesse being taken away. I did not know it at the time but I had fallen into a depression although I had not really shown extreme signs of it. My grades falling, my lack of wanting to dress up for school, withdrawing from friends — all of that was part of my depression.

Those were the first signs of the worst of my depression that would come in later years. Since I had never spoken to anyone about what I had been through, nor had I expressed my feelings of hurt, pain, confusion, anger, sadness and hopelessness, they played themselves out in the form of what I was experiencing. At the time the only person I could cling to was Jesse. A few days after the car had been taken from me and I had to come home right after school, I was in my room and a complete sadness and loneliness came over me. A kind of sadness that felt like it would never go away. So bad that I felt the only way I could ever feel better or not feel it at all was to end my life. I had threatened once before to end my life.

I was about nine years old and living with my older sister while my mother was in rehab. She and her boyfriend had promised me that we would all go to the beach the next day as a family. I went to bed that night super excited to go to the beach and when I awoke the next day, I awoke to the news that we would not be going after all. I was so disappointed that I locked myself in the bathroom and drew many pictures of sand and water. I covered the bathroom floor with those pictures and cried. When the crying did not help and the pain was too much to bear I looked in the cabinet to see if we had any pills I could swallow. I don't know where I learned that I could die from swallowing pills; it must have been TV, but the bottom-line was that I knew. I looked in the medicine cabinet and found nothing but makeup and some cotton swabs. I knew there was no way I would die on lipstick and ear cleaners so I did the only thing I could think of to ease the pain; I cried myself to sleep on the bathroom floor. No one came to look for me.

That was my first attempt or thought of suicide. Now I was older and wiser, and that night that same pain came over me once again, but more intense. Somehow, after all that had happened to me, I had been able to hide the pain, to suppress the hurt, fear and anger. I hid in my closet and pretended to enter an imaginary world; I left my body and my spirit soared over magical places. I dreamt myself near beaches or on islands with many animals. Now at fifteen, I had lost that imagination. My innocence, my will to go on, something in my soul. I was tired. Tired of living. I walked into our bathroom and locked the door behind me. My mother was watching TV in the back room and my stepfather in his. They would be too involved with their favorite shows to notice that I would be ending my life that night.

I looked at myself in the mirror with no thought other than, "I was tired and I was ready to go." I saw my face and it looked haggard and sad. There was no hesitation in what I was about to do. I had nothing to live for anymore. Without thought or feeling, I opened the medicine cabinet where I knew we kept the Tylenol and poured what was left in it. Half a bottle of pills. I don't remember exactly how many just that they all fit in the cup of my hand. Without hesitation I swallowed them all. A faint thought of "What did you just do Alicia?" came to me, but the second thought was the one that I held on to — "I will go soon and all this torturous life will be over."

I opened the door, went back to my room and laid down. I closed my eyes and tried very hard to take myself back to that imaginary world that I had gone to as a child. The world where animals roamed free and all of them got along. Where love was plentiful and everything around me made me feel safe. I wanted to go to sleep just like what I had seen in the movies. People overdose with pills, they lie down, fall asleep and within a few minutes they are peacefully gone. That scenario ran through my head and nothing else. The emotional pain was so intense that the thought of leaving the people I loved the most was not a concern. I just wanted the pain to go away. As life would have it, I quickly realized that movies were not always what happens in real life.

A few minutes after I had swallowed a handful of pills, I began to feel queasy and dizzy. My stomach began to bloat and a sharp pain made me cringe into a fetal position. The magical place I was in was gone and I was back to reality. I had a severe stomach pain and ready to throw up. I must have been ten minutes into swallowing the pills when I had to get myself to the bathroom to vomit. I felt as if I could vomit everything I had eaten that day and my intestines along with my organs would come out too. My head was throbbing and the dizziness became worse. I stumbled to the bathroom, where I pushed the door open and fell to my knees, above the toilet seat.

In my haste to reach the toilet bowl, I did not close the bathroom door behind me so the sound of me throwing up caught my mother's and stepfather's attention. My sounds must have been horrifying because my mother was yelling at the top of her lungs that she was rushing a glass of water to me. I vomited the pills first. I remember the bitter burning taste of the pills coming up my stomach, through my esophagus and out of my mouth leaving the acidic aftertaste along the way. The taste and smell added to my discomfort and threw up the rest of whatever was in my stomach. After I was done throwing up, I continued with liquid and saliva. I could not stop and my stomach and head were throbbing. Somehow, during all of the commotion, I must have told my mother that I had swallowed the pills because before I knew it the paramedics, police and ambulance were in my house and I was being wheeled out on a gurney. It was late at night, but that did not stop the spectators from crowding around my house. I was sure they were wondering if law enforcement were there because my mother had gone back to her old ways. As they wheeled me out, it was clear that that was not the case. Instead, her daughter was the one in trouble.

As if I had not been excluded enough at school, this would be the straw that would break the camel's back. The entire school would really ignore me now. I was rushed to the hospital and during the ambulance ride I was asked many questions. "What kind of pills did I take and how many?' and "Why had I done this." I could not process what they were saying. None of what they asked made sense because my head was still throbbing and I was still trying to make sense of what had happened. I never thought myself brave enough or stupid enough to actually go through with committing suicide. I could not understand it myself so their asking questions when I was in so much pain was useless. I could not say a word.

When I arrived at the hospital, I was rushed into the emergency room to pump my stomach clean. As if I was not in pain enough the pumps were the final torture for me. They stuck a tube down my nose and into my throat, a thick long clear tube. I had no pain medication and no anesthesia to put me to sleep; they wasted no time and stuffed it down my nostril, past my throat and into my stomach. At the same time, they were inserting needles in my arms, checking my blood pressure, temperature and heartbeat. All of this commotion was going on and I could not say a word. The doctor proceeded to pump black tar into my stomach. As it traveled down my nose, through my throat and into my stomach, it felt very warm and painful. I could not decide which was worse, the pain of the pumps or the pain in my throat of the tar slowly flowing down my esophagus. The acid from all the vomiting at home had left it raw and tender and now this made it worse. The taste of the tar was a whole new experience; I wanted to throw up once again. Once the black tar entered my stomach it settled for a few seconds and just as they expected, I began to vomit it out. It felt like this nightmare would never end. After a few minutes, I endured the last of the vomiting and pain from this cleansing. The doctor pulled the tube out of my stomach, through my nose. I felt like I was about to faint from the experience. They allowed me to rest for a few hours before someone came to speak with me. I took advantage of those few minutes to think about what I would say. How would I explain the reasoning behind my suicide attempt? I thought and thought and I could not come up with a good explanation. I could not explain it because I did not know why myself.

At the time all I knew was that I was in pain, and I was tired. I was not aware that I had fallen into a deep depression. I had no clue what was wrong with me so I could not ask for help, nor could I explain why I swallowed many pills in an attempt to end my life. Between thinking and staring at the ceiling I would doze on and off. I was so tired. I had nurses come check on me periodically so sleeping through the night was not possible. My mom was not allowed to visit me until I spoke with a social worker the following morning. I guess whatever I told the social worker made her believe that I was no longer a danger to myself.

I was discharged the following day and my mother and Jesse came to get me. Neither one asked me questions about what I had done. They did ask how I was feeling. We pretended nothing had happened and went to eat at a restaurant. I guess they did not realize that that was my cry for help. Once again, they missed an opportunity to ask me what was wrong, to really dig deep and ask why I had done this. I guess it was easier for everyone, including my sisters, to ignore my suicide attempt. They had already dealt with so much in the past this was not another thing they could handle. I tried very hard to hide that event of my life, to pretend it never happened. We never talked about it again.

Chapter 16

I Swear, It was the Food

A few months later we decided to take a trip to Las Vegas. Visiting Las Vegas had become a regular outing for us. My mother would often take me with her and friends on road trips to Las Vegas. She and my aunt loved to gamble, so anytime someone offered her a free ride to Sin City, she would not say no. I remember being younger, maybe seven or eight and going to the city that never sleeps; the road trip up there was long and hot. Most of the time the car or van we were traveling in did not have air conditioning, so we had to deal with the heat as best we could. Usually it meant drinking a cold soda or just leaving the windows open to feel the warm breeze. I would sit and look out the window into a sea of nothing but desert. Once there, the adults would take turns watching the children in the pool or in the hotel room while the other adults went out to gamble.

On our way out of the hotel, my mother would have me sit next to her at a slot machine and watch as she would insert quarters in hopes of winning money. I would sit there until the security guard would come and ask us to leave. Then she would find a spot for me, in some corner, away from the slot machines and say, "*No te muevas de aquí, que ahorita vengo.*" She basically told me not to move in Spanish. I always did what she said, not so much out of respect but out of fear that I would become lost in the sea of slot machines and people. I would wait half an hour at the most until it was time for all of us to go meet up and go home. This time, however, we were not going with friends, but with my sisters. By this time my middle sister had her son who was about seven and my oldest sister was pregnant with her oldest son.

During our road trip, I became very nauseous. We had stopped for some hot dogs and a few hours later that hot dog came right back out. My middle sister had to stop the car so that I could throw up everything I had eaten at the rest stop. "She must have eaten something bad," was the only thing my mother could think of at the time. Little did we all know, especially me, that it was not the food that had caused my nausea. I can't talk about the rest of the ride nor the trip itself because my memory stops there.

A few days later, back at home, I found out that I was pregnant. I don't remember how I found out but one thing I do remember was that I needed to let my mother know. Many thoughts raced through my mind, "Should I keep this baby." I thought about it for a while and Jesse and I discussed this considerably. There were times when he and I would have conversations about having a child. I really wanted to have someone to love and who would love me back. Many nights I thought about creating my own family since I felt that I did not have one of my own. My family was so dysfunctional that maybe having my own child would create that stability and the sense of belonging to a family that I craved so much.

This baby was really planned as I knew what I was doing at sixteen. I understood the consequences of making adult decisions. What I did not understand were all the responsibilities and life changes that would come with having a child. "It did not seem so hard to be a mother. Families are beautiful and I can have one of my own. Jesse and I can rent a house and live happily ever after, like in the movies." These thoughts permeated my soul. My longing for a family and happy life with children, a husband and a white picket fence was what my soul was craving. What I wanted now I almost had. I was a mother to an unborn child. As I talked to Jesse we decided to let my middle sister know first. I figured she would tell my mother (she could never keep a secret) and then it would be easier for me not to say anything. I was afraid to tell my mom. I knew that she would be disappointed in me. She had stopped drinking to make sure I had a better life. She would pay me money each time I received good grades and she would talk about me as if I would be someone successful one day. My older sister had instilled the fact that I would be the first in our family to go to college and actually graduate. Being pregnant would greatly disappoint her.

I looked up to my older sister. She was married now and had her own beautiful home in Sylmar. She had a beautiful baby boy and was expecting another one. She would often throw parties and I enjoyed going over and spending time with her and my nephew.

Jesse and I went over to Veronica's house and told her I was expecting. We told her our plans to keep the baby and to find a home for ourselves. When I arrived back home after the talk with my sister, my mother called me to the kitchen. That must have been the fastest my sister had ever passed any news to my mother. It had not even been an hour after I had left her house when my mom asked to speak with me. "Alicia, *ven*." I walked as slowly as I could to the kitchen because I knew exactly what she was going to ask. "*Estas embarazada*." "Yes, mom." I responded with much regret. I could not look at her. She began to cry. I had only seen my mother cry out of real sadness twice before, the day I was taken away from her and the day I was in court and on the witness stand. This would be the third time I would see her cry out of sadness and it made me cry too. A sense of shame overtook me and lowered my head. I could not bear to see her cry again.

After I admitted that I was pregnant and my mother had stopped crying, she began to ask questions. "*Porque?*" "I don't know Mom, it just happened." I wish I could remember the rest of her reaction. I want to say that she cussed me out and called me every name in the book, but I don't know because I have blocked that memory out.

In the next few days, she sat with me and said that I would have to drop out of school and take care of this child. She said it in such a way that I did not have any choice. She wanted me to make sure I went to the Welfare office, the government assistance office, to let them know I was pregnant. "They will give you the money and food you need so you don't have to work or go to school and you can stay home with your child." During this time my mother was receiving welfare for me as she had for my other two sisters since they were born and until they turned eighteen. Even though she had worked at times the government still gave her money. So working was always a choice for her. I was still under age, so she would get food stamps and money from the government.

As soon as she uttered the words, "Stay home and drop out," I felt blood rush to my face and anger set in. First off, I could not see myself accepting money from anyone. I had worked since the age of fifteen and was very capable of continuing to work. Also, I did not see myself dropping out of school. School had saved me once before, and it would again. I would focus on school and do well for me and this baby. I was angry. Who was she to tell me what I was or was not going to do? I was going to stay in school and she was not going to change my mind. I was sixteen, pregnant, and going to school.

Chapter 17

I Can't Do This

I figured having a baby would not be that bad. I had had responsibilities before, and I was good at them. Well, almost good at them. At fifteen, I was hired for my first job. I was a clerk in a video rental store. I loved the job. I would check out videos, clean the store, restock returned videos and check out customers. I made sure I worked as hard as I could. I remember my mother saying, "Don't let me see you standing around, always make sure you stay busy." So that's exactly what I would do. If we did not have customers, I would clean or vacuum the store. Within two weeks the owners gave me a 50-cent raise. I was ecstatic. I felt so honored to have the owners acknowledge my hard work. I felt important and special. They soon promoted me to manager and I would open or close the store by myself. I felt like an adult because adults trusted me with their livelihood.

This business was the main source of income for the business owners and they trusted me enough to run it. Jesse would come around during the times I was by myself and he would often accompany me. He would watch me make the cash transactions. One day he asked me to take money out of the cash register and give it to him. "Don't worry, no one will notice," he said. I felt my stomach shrink in fear and sadness at the thought that I would be taking money that did not belong to me. I was in love and I wanted to please Jesse. Against my morals and knowing what I was doing was wrong, I took five dollars out of the cash register and gave it to him. I went back and made sure there were no receipts to show that there had been money there. I did it once, twice, and as I did it again, it became easier.

They say you become what you do, and I had become a thief. I was ashamed of myself and every time I did it I lost self-respect. My self-esteem and my identity were slowly being ripped from my very existence. I was losing more of myself and more of my soul. But in my desperate need to be loved by Jesse, I complied. I had no more voice, I could not stand my ground.

I lost my job when the owners noticed that money had been missing. I was called into the office and they were blunt about the situation. "Alicia, we know you have been stealing money. "You are fired." That tore my heart to pieces. I betrayed the people who trusted me. More than that I had betrayed myself, again. "Had I not learned from the guilt I carried from stealing the stickers from the church long ago?" Obviously, I had not. My first job and I did something horrible. I did not admit to it, instead I said "Okay." And with my head down I walked out of my first job; a job that gave me some identity, some self-esteem and some self-worth.

As soon as I stepped out of the store, I realized I had lost more than just a job.

After that I worked at a Dollar Store as a clerk and sometimes I would go with Jesse to sell tennis shoes at the swap-meet. Somehow or other I always had money. I worked hard and tried to right the wrong that I had done. So now I was standing there with my mother saying how I had to drop out of school and not work so that I could live on government assistance and take care of my child. This was not how I had planned things. I was supposed to go to college, not drop out of high school. I went back to my room and cried. I cried out of sadness and confusion. I cried because I did not know what to do.

That was when the thought of terminating my pregnancy crossed my mind. "I am not ready to have a baby. I am not ready to leave school. I want to go to college. I'm scared I won't be a good mother. I was only sixteen. I made up my mind that night that I would terminate the pregnancy. My mother thought it would be best. I made an appointment and the lady on the phone asked me if I was sure. "You're very far along you know. It will require for us to perform it in two days." She explained the procedure. It seemed horrible.

Too horrible for me to even discuss in this book. I went through with setting up the appointment.

Miracles happen because the appointment she gave was not until the following week. Those days made me think and rethink what she said about the procedure. I shared it with my mom and she seemed uneasy about it. I thought about this baby in my womb and I thought about my life. It was overwhelming. I did not really talk to anyone about my feelings, not even Jesse. He was fine with whatever decision I made. I guess his family had talked to him about the cons of having a child now because at first he had been excited too. The night before my appointment something happened to both my mother and to me.

My aunt called and spoke to me about me keeping the baby. I guess that's all I needed. I just wanted someone to say, "It's going to be okay." We were at Veronica's house because she was the one who was going to take me to the clinic. My mother sat down on the bed and told me that she did not want me to terminate this pregnancy. "I will help you raise this child. We will do whatever it takes to make sure you and this baby are fine. Just don't do it." Those words were music to my ears. I felt such a weight off my shoulders, a darkness and sadness had been lifted. Peace had entered my heart.

I did not think twice to change my decision. I went back to El Monte the following day with my mom. She decided not to let my stepfather know at the time. I did not question it. I figured out of respect that I lived under his roof it would be best. He did not really like Jesse that much. The news that I was expecting a child with Jesse would disappoint him, to say the least.

I am sure there were many reasons why my mother did not want to tell him. She probably did not want to hear him say, "I told you so. That kid is bad news." Even though he was not my biological father, I had grown up with him and we had a bond, not a close one but he still loved me in his own way. Like any parent, he too would be disappointed.

I went back to school as usual and did not say anything. I hid my pregnancy from friends and my stepfather. I wore baggy clothes to cover my growing belly. My family and I did not talk about me being pregnant. I figured that we did not discuss it because of the shame that my mother felt about the whole situation. I felt the same way. Although my mother and I agreed for me to have this child, we were still in denial. I was hiding my pregnancy from myself too. I kept to myself in my room most of the time. I would come home from school and go into my room. Many times I actually forgot I was pregnant because I did not have any pregnancy symptoms other than being sleepy. I did everything I normally did, including washing and waxing my car at midnight. I would usually do that out of anxiety.

I went with my friends to a carnival once during my fourth month of pregnancy. I had not shared with the few friends I had the fact that I was pregnant, so we all bought tickets for this pretty intense carnival ride. As I was standing in line I read the warning, "If you have back or neck problems or if you are pregnant, you should not ride this ride." I read it twice hoping the warning would magically disappear. I really wanted to ride the ride. I thought about ignoring the warning sign, "I'm sure it's no big deal if I get on the ride" I thought. But my gut said otherwise. I could not ignore this sign. For the last four months I had been wearing baggy clothes and not talking about my pregnancy. I did not feel pregnant and I did not think about the baby in my womb. I had not bought baby clothes nor did I read books about motherhood or babies. I had been given information at my doctor's office, but I never really took the time to read them. Jesse and I did not talk about it either. We did not talk about the future, nor about the baby. Days kind of just passed along.

That night I just wanted to be normal. I wanted to fit in and not think about being pregnant. As I was standing in line all I could think about was how I was carrying this baby inside my body. I thought about the warning sign and how it could affect my baby. It just did not feel right. A few minutes after standing in line, I told my friends that I was scared and I would not ride. They did not have a problem with it and I walked down the stairs to wait for them. The decision made me feel good. The rest of the evening was fun. I enjoyed my time being a teenager, forgetting I was pregnant — for the time being.

Chapter 18

Baby on TV

Around my sixth month of pregnancy, I went to my doctor's appointment. I still was not showing at all. My regular shorts and pants still fit. A few weeks before my appointment, I had been watching lots of talk shows. That was pretty much all I had the motivation to do. On one of those shows there was a couple with a child who was born with Down's syndrome. They discussed how difficult it was to raise this baby whose disability kept him and his parents from enjoying a normal life. That show made a huge impact on me. "What if my child were born with Down's Syndrome? What would I do?" I was freaked out. The thought of something being wrong with my child scared me to death. "Was this baby okay?" I had to know.

During the visit to my doctor, I asked him about Down's syndrome. He stated that it was most likely to occur in older parents, "Mothers over 30," he said. "Unless it runs in the family. If you have someone in the family who has it might be passed on." I thought for a quick second and I could not think of anyone in my immediate family who had it. My sisters seemed fine. My mother had mentioned a few times that my aunt on my father's side had a child with Down's syndrome. I could not remember if she said it was from lack of oxygen during childbirth or that the child was born with it. I did not want to take a chance of not knowing if my child was okay. "It runs in my family," I said without hesitation. "Your mother or father's side," he asked. "My father's side," I quickly responded. I was not sure and it was not like I could call my father anytime. He left when I was six months old never to be seen again. The best I could do was to tell the doctor what my mother had said. "I will set up for an ultrasound next week to see if anything is abnormal," he said. After he measured my stomach, he saw that there was no growth of my belly; that gave him the motivation to test right away.

As I walked out of the doctor's office, I looked around and saw all the other pregnant women in the waiting area, and they actually looked pregnant. Some had small bellies and others really large ones. Not me. I barely had a bump. So the following week I went to have the ultrasound done. I went by myself again. Jesse had been working and was given odd and long hours. "Ms. Leon," the ultrasound doctor called me in. All this was new to me. Hesitantly and a little nervous, I walked into the patient room. I saw a huge machine and a hospital bed next to it. The doctor explained the procedure and asked me to change into the hospital gown. It felt a little awkward to have to undress and show my belly to some stranger. I laid down and he proceeded to rub this cold, clear gel over my belly. He explained that he would take a few pictures and then it would be over. I did not see the baby on the monitor. I don't know why the doctor did not show it to me. He must have thought I was too young or maybe he did not approve of young mothers. The whole process felt so cold and sad.

I went back to see my regular doctor a few days later and he gave me the news that apparently something was wrong with my baby. "Your baby is not growing the normal way a baby should grow. The baby should be much bigger for the months along you have," he said. "This could be a sign of Down's Syndrome." I could not have been more devastated. My worst fear was about to be confirmed. "We will have to perform an amniocentesis. "An amnio-cent-what?" I could not even say the name of what he had to do. "We have to insert a needle into your stomach and into the baby's amniotic fluid sac. We have to take a sample of the fluid and run tests to see if your child has Down's. We will check for other illnesses as well. What we do is check to make sure your child has all the normal chromosomes. If one set of chromosomes is off, then something is wrong and we will know." His words were coming to me way too fast and all I understood was that they felt my child had Down's syndrome and they would have to poke through my stomach to check.

I was shocked. The doctor sensed this and was quick to give me my options. He knew I would go home and have questions. He continued to tell me that if the test came back positive, I had the choice of keeping my child or terminating the pregnancy. I had the choice again to end my child's life if that's what I wanted. He explained that the procedure would take two days to complete since I was far along. He did not go into details, but I already knew the process as that had been an option from the beginning. I could not believe I would have to deal with having to make a decision like that again. The first time had been torture. I couldn't' say anything, I was speechless.

I drove straight home after that appointment and spoke with Jesse and my mom about it. Jesse did not say anything. I think he was shocked as well. He did say he would go with me to the appointment. My mother on the other hand did not hesitate to say I should terminate the pregnancy if something was wrong. "Don't take any chances," she said. "Life is hard enough for normal people and if you bring a child with special needs into the world you and that child will suffer tremendously." Hearing those words only made it worse.

I was torn, not sure what to think or do. Part of me wanted this baby. I had already felt it move in my belly. Little butterflies floating around were what it felt like. Yet, part of me did not want to deal with a child with special needs. How would I handle it and, what would people think of my child? People would judge and stare. I went to bed that night exhausted and emotionally drained. This was by far more information than a sixteen-year old could handle. I felt too immature to understand it all. I felt I was just going through the motions of breathing but I was not really living. I was not experiencing the joy of pregnancy the way the commercials or sitcoms showed. I was not sharing my happy experiences with people the way other pregnant women did.

I went to bed that night without any space for one more thought other than I needed sleep. Sleep was often the only way I was able to leave the stress and sadness I felt. I once again began trying to control my dreams and imagined myself anywhere I wanted to be. I tried to take myself to my imaginary heaven that I had created as a child. But that heaven was not there anymore.

A few days later, Jesse picked me up for my appointment. I expected the worse. Jesse and I did not speak on the way, silence seemed perfect for the situation. We arrived at the doctor's office and anxiously sat in the waiting room. I did not know what to expect nor could I envision how the procedure would go. After what seemed like hours, the nurse called us in. Jesse looked very nervous and was not his usual self. I became even more nervous. The nurse led us into a what looked like an emergency surgery room. There was a hospital bed and alongside it a small table with a blue plastic cloth and some doctor tools. I glanced once and then a second time because I thought I had seen a knife as part of the tool package. I was wrong, thank goodness.

Jesse found a chair next to the hospital bed and sat down. The doctor noticed our nervousness and broke the ice by saying something funny, I did not know what he meant but out of courtesy I laughed. He then proceeded to tell us what he would be doing. "You will need to change into this hospital gown and lie on the bed. I will numb your stomach area, then I will carefully insert a needle into your stomach. It will go into the bag where the fetus is, the womb. I will be looking at the fetus the whole time as I am inserting the needle, to make sure I don't poke the fetus."

The way he kept saying fetus was so cold. I thought it was a baby. "We will be able to see what is happening in that TV monitor." He pointed to a television screen just above the bed. I could not believe that as I had scanned the room, I had missed the huge television mounted on the wall. "I will leave you now to get ready, and I will be back in a few minutes to begin the amniocentesis." After the doctor had left the room, I explained to Jesse what he had said. I was sure that it had been too much information for him to take in at once; he also struggled understanding some English words. His only response was silence. I guess he understood.

I changed into the gown and lay down on the bed. A knock at the door and the doctor came in. "I will rub some alcohol on your stomach first and then an orange solution." I took turns watching the TV monitor that he had turned on and looking at him. There was a nurse behind him, making sure he had everything he needed. Then he rubbed some clear jelly-like substance on one area of my stomach and ran a small scanner over that area. I looked at the TV monitor just at the moment when a clear picture of my baby had come to view. It was black and white and looked like a shadowed outline. The fetus, as the doctor had called it, had a shape and it looked like a baby all curled up. The head, the tiny arms and legs and fingers. It seemed so surreal.

I could not believe that's what was growing in my stomach. I was mesmerized by the image of my baby.

I turned to look at Jesse as I wanted to see his reaction, but he simply had a blank stare on his face. I quickly turned back as I did not want to lose this beautiful sight. Many emotions came flooding all at once. I was drowned in amazement yet pitted with feelings of guilt at the same time. There was a real baby and I had not spoken to it. Not once had I acknowledged its presence. I had been hiding it the whole time, pretending it was not there. No baby songs, no baby clothes, no touching my belly in a sweet and loving way, nothing.

"Okay, I am going to insert the needle now. I found a good place to take some fluid out." The doctor's words broke the flow of emotions and brought me back to the moment. I turned and looked at the large needle he was about to insert and my heart sank. It must have been at least twelve inches long and pretty sharp. I usually was not afraid of needles, but this one made my intestines curl up real quick. I took a long hard breath and held it as he inserted the needle just above my belly button. I looked up at the monitor and saw the picture of the needle going in, just missing my baby by a few centimeters. It wasn't there long, just enough for him to withdraw some fluid to test. I did not feel any pain. The numbing lotion he had rubbed on me worked well. Within seconds he had pulled the needle out and instructed the nurse to clean up my stomach. "You're all done," he said. "We will call you with the results in about two weeks." He turned and walked out of the room

Before the nurse could get to me, I heard her say, "Sir, are you alright? Sir?" I turned to look at Jesse when I realized she was talking to him. His face began to turn a pale yellow and then a milky white. Within seconds he began to sway from side to side, he was about to pass out. The nurse quickly ran to him and held him up. I could not do anything but stare. I had never seen a person pass out before. The nurse rushed toward him and grabbed him before he fell. He was given a glass of water. I looked and him and I asked if he was okay. "Yes, I am fine," he said. He didn't look fine to me. As he regained all color, I quickly changed into my clothes. We walked out of the patient room and into the waiting room, all the while the doctors were asking how he was feeling. He repeated, "I am okay." He drank his glass of water and left.

During the whole drive home, he could not stop talking about how long and sharp the needle was and how he felt pain at the sight of it. Funny how he felt the pain, the needle was not anywhere near him. At that point I realized what a chicken he was with needles.

That following week proved to be bittersweet. I received a phone call from the doctor's office stating that they had the results of the test. I remember clearly the day the phone rang. That whole week I had been anxiously awaiting the results, my stomach in knots and my mind in a haze, hoping that all would be well, that my child would be healthy and normal. I chose not to think about what I would do if the results came out positive for Down's syndrome. The thought of the results led me back to the conversation with my mother. "You can't bring a child with disabilities into this world," she said. "It's bad enough that this world is cruel and vicious; you have vultures and thieves waiting to eat you alive in this world." As much as I wanted to disagree with her, I could not. Life had been hard on me and I had seen the vultures and thieves she had talked about. I had experienced it for myself and every day the news reminded me of just how horrible human beings could be to each other. Murders, robberies, deaths, suicides, war, diseases, hatred, bullying, neglect were all part of this world and to bring a child into it would be selfish.

Bringing a child with disabilities into this world would be extremely unfair to the baby. I also knew that I did not want to deal with a child with disabilities for many selfish reasons. "How would I take care of him or her? Who would help me? What kind of life would he or she have? The thoughts that were the most selfish were, "How will people judge me? They will make fun of my child and of me." I cared so much about how people would treat me and talk about me that I forgot that I would bring a loving soul into the world which would be unique and special in his or her own way.

When the call came I anxiously picked up the phone and heard the doctor's voice. "Ms. Leon, hi, this is Doctor Smith." She said it in such a happy tone that I knew everything was fine. She continued describing the results, but I was not processing any of it. I was just waiting for the part where she would say it was good. After a few minutes she finally said it. Her words were clear as day, "The results show that your baby is perfectly normal." Oh, the relief that I felt. Finally, I could go back to hiding my pregnancy and ignoring life as it was. What caught me off guard however was that she had called the fetus a baby. The other doctor had called it a fetus. She continued with a question that was totally unexpected, "Would you like to know the sex of your baby?" I couldn't believe that I could know at that moment the gender of my baby. I paused for a few seconds and said "Yes." Part of me did not want to know but the maternal instinct in me did.

"Well," she said, "Congratulations, it's a girl." My heart stopped. Time stopped. All I could say was "thank you." I hung up the phone. I sat there and looked at my mother as she waited for the results from me. *"Está bien y va a ser niña."* I said. My mother had already been babysitting my one-year old nephew from my older sister and my middle sister also had a son, so underneath it all my mother was happy. She was happy that I was having a girl but she sure did not show it that day. *"Que bueno"* were the only words she uttered as she went back into the kitchen to tend to my nephew. I went back to my room and fell asleep.

The following month was the usual. Every day was the same. I woke up, ate breakfast and watched TV. I was tired of being home, but I did not have a choice. After a few weeks of bed rest at the request of my doctor, my stomach was beginning to get bigger so decided to pull myself out of my regular high school to attend the teen pregnancy school. I no longer had my regular high school friends because by this time they all knew of my pregnancy and decided or maybe their parents decided that I was not a good person to hang around with. I lost the few friends I had made. I did not see Jesse much, so I was home most of the time. Any chance I had to go out I would take even if it meant just going to the drugstore to buy mundane items like toilet paper. Anything to get me out of the house.

One day my mother decided to go to the store to buy groceries. I saw her walk out the back and walk past the side of the house. I noticed her because I had been in the living room next to the window watching television. I quickly jumped up and asked her where she was going. *"A dónde vas?"* I asked. "Oh, just to the store." She said in Spanish. "Wait for me, I'll put on my shoes and go with you." "You don't have to," she quickly responded. "Maybe you should stay home and rest." "No, it's okay, I want to go." I saw some hesitation in her face and her voice mumbled something I did not quite comprehend. I saw her turn around and thought she would wait for me. Instead, she said he would just go later. I knew then why she changed her mind. All this time she had me hiding my pregnancy because she was ashamed of me. All this time she never once offered to buy baby clothes with me or ask how I was doing. She did not offer to take me pregnancy clothes shopping. I had to buy regular clothes just a size bigger each time. She did not talk to me about how to be a parent or what I would expect from pregnancy.

This day she showed how embarrassed she was to be seen with me. During my childhood, I had been embarrassed of my mother and now the tables had turned. I wish I could say that I felt sad and ashamed, but the negative feelings I felt towards myself transcended sadness and shame. Truly, there are no words to capture the heart wrenching feeling of your only parent shaming you in such a cruel way.

I had enrolled myself in a teen pregnancy school and would drive myself there every day. It felt nice to be around other teenage girls, knowing that I was not alone. I felt blessed that such a program existed, not only so that I could socialize with other teen moms, but I learned a lot about being a parent. I learned things like how my body was changing and how my emotions would change too. I also learned how to properly change a diaper and what to do when my child would cry. Even though I would find myself lost when the actual time came for me to care for my daughter, the immediate sense of thinking I was proficient put me at ease.

Around my seventh month of pregnancy, I could no longer hide my stomach as it had grown what seemed like overnight. My mother finally broke the news to my stepfather (I wasn't there when it happened) and he was not happy about it. He was good at hiding his emotions, but I do remember my mother saying that it had been her fault for allowing me to see him with such freedom. My stepfather never said anything to me. We didn't have a bond that allowed us to speak with each other comfortably. Everything that he was unhappy with he would bring it up to my mother's attention, never to me.

Chapter 19

Nurse, Please Take the Baby!

J esse and I continued seeing each other. We traveled to Arizona on short vacations and talked about what our future would be like when the baby came. We figured that we move out on our own to raise the baby. Around my eighth month of pregnancy, we set out searching for a place that would be affordable for a sixteen and nineteen-year old. I was not working, but I was receiving government assistance and Jesse had a minimum wage job working at the local supermarket. We looked at many places, but they were too expensive. We finally came upon some apartments across a high school not too far from my mom's house. They are known as the Mildred Apartments and were considered to be low income housing where there were lots of turmoil. Gangs roamed the area and there was a lot of alcohol use there. I was not aware of this at the time. When we went to look at them, the complex seemed quiet and safe. Most importantly, it was near my mom's home.

We signed the paperwork and moved in. We took a bed and some light furniture. I don't think we had a television. I spent most of the day with my mom and would come back at night. I began to notice people drinking outside the apartments and smoking. People would stare at Jesse and me as we would go in and I felt creeped out by the whole place. I was young and this had been the first time I had been out on my own. As I got closer to my due date, the day I was to give birth, I noticed I had not even fixed the crib. The baby crib had been given to me at the baby shower that Jesse's aunt had given me. It was still full of all the gifts that I had not bothered to open. I was not prepared having this baby.

Mentally, I had not bonded with my child and I was not in the mood to decorate or prepare her living area. Nothing was ready for her. I was beginning to fall deeper into my depression, I think. I was beginning to hate the apartment. Every day, more and more roaches would come out. I would see more and more drinking and loitering in the apartments. I was scared when I left the apartment and I was scared when I came back. Jesse would come home at night and I would tell him how much I wanted to move out. I hated it there. It did not feel like a home. Especially with the racket the next door neighbors made with their loud music and all night drinking. Each time he would convince me to stay.

One night after another heated discussion on moving, I finally gave up on the idea when, toward the middle of the night, I began feeling back pain. My back pain began to increase around two in the morning. Jesse rubbed my back, in the hope that it would ease my pain, but it did not help. I cried and cried. I did not realize I was having labor pains. I thought I was sleeping wrong. Around five in the morning my back pain turned into sharp pains in my stomach. I called my mother and she said most likely I was in labor and would have to go to the hospital. I was on Medical, a government issued insurance. I was told by my primary care doctor that I would have to go to a certain hospital located in East Los Angeles. I got up, showered and headed that way. The car ride to the hospital was not that bad. I was in pain, but it was bearable. It felt like intense cramping but enough to hold a conversation with Jesse. We decided that since it was not so bad we would make a stop to see my sister Veronica. We sat in her living room for a while and talked and when my pains began to get stronger we decided to leave. This time my pains had increased and I went into intense crying. It was an indescribable pain. Knives cutting through my stomach is the best way to describe it.

We arrived at the hospital that I had been assigned to. It was a small and very dim and dark looking hospital. I was taken into a room that was the size of my bathroom. It had but a chair and the bed I was on. I lay on the bed in pain and Jesse sat on the chair. I cried and yelled, only to have a nurse come and ask me to "Please be quiet." I was not given ice or water to help quench my thirst, and they didn't hook me up to any monitors to check my condition or that of my baby. I was extremely distressed. I did not know what was happening and no one was telling me anything. Jesse had no clue what to do either. I asked him to call my older sister because no one was saying anything. He called her and gave me the phone. In between pain spurts she made sure to tell me that I had the right to go to any hospital of my choice if I was not being properly taken care of there. I got up, changed and left the hospital without saying anything to the nurses. Jesse drove me to the Queen of the Valley Hospital in West Covina. On the way my pains got worse. I could no longer sit properly and I was yelling and crying non-stop.

Upon arrival at the hospital, I was unable to get out of the car, so the nurse had to bring a wheelchair for me. Even sitting on the wheelchair was difficult. I was immediately taken into a room. The hospital looked like a real hospital, brightly lit, nurses walking around and doctors available. I noticed those things even though I was in excruciating pain. I was lying on the bed screaming, hoping that it would all be over soon, when a nurse came in and asked that I keep it down. "Keep it down?" Didn't she know I was in a lot of pain? I felt like someone was tearing into my stomach with knives and ripping my intestines apart. "Please give me medicine," I begged. She left the room and came back with a syringe. "You're almost ready to deliver, so this is the only thing I can give you." She proceeded to inject me with Demerol. Demerol was a medicine to put your body at ease. Problem was it made me drowsy. For a while, I felt as if I was at a restaurant. I heard the clanking of metal spoons and forks and heard people talking over food. I heard waiters waiting on people. This "medicine" was more of a drug and not a good one. I was out of it.

A few moments later, I was in the delivery room and I remember Jesse being there as well. The doctor kept asking me to push but I could not. I was so drugged out. I was not fully aware of my surroundings or what was going on. I tried to follow his instructions, but my body wouldn't respond. "Push." He yelled again. I tried and tried. "Give me the suction, I will have to suction this baby out." She was almost out but would be stuck in the birth canal unless he acted quickly. So he did what he had to do and my daughter came out, took her first breath and cried a little. I remember feeling such a sense of relief from the whole ordeal. I was relieved from the pushing and pain, but most of all from hearing the doctor scream at me to push. I remember feeling my stomach so empty. Something was missing. It felt hollow. I looked at my daughter and her dad taking pictures and that's all I remember.

I awoke shortly after in my hospital room. Jesse was there and stayed for a while, long enough for my grogginess to dissipate somewhat. He had things to do so he left. A few minutes after he left the nurse came in with my daughter in her plastic rolling crib. Through the glass I could see a small bundle rolled up like a burrito in the center of the crib. Around her were diapers and bottles of milk. "Will you be nursing?" asked the nurse. "I am not sure, "I said. "Well, you have to make up your mind really quick. She will be hungry soon." I watched her leave and was unsure why she did not take the baby with her. Why did she leave the crib with the baby in the room? I was about to yell out to her, "You forgot to take the baby." But before I could utter those words, she was gone and I was left there with this "baby."

I still had not come to terms with the fact that she was mine. She seemed like a stranger. I did not know this baby and she did not know me either. "What am I going to do with her now" were the thoughts that raced through my head. I was alone and had no clue what to do. I guess the teen pregnancy school had not trained me as well as I thought they did. I laid back on my hospital bed trying not to think about this baby next to my bed. I was still in denial about her birth and thinking about it only made her more real. I turned sideways as to not face the crib and closed my eyes. Sleep. Sleep is really all I wanted. Sleep was the only thing that removed me from the reality of my problems and put me in a place where I could be somewhere else or someone else. My dreams were what I always counted on to make me feel better. Not my nightmares, but my dreams. I closed my eyes in the hope that I would dream myself away to some beautiful place; anywhere but here.

I must have slept for a few minutes when I awoke to the sound of a baby crying. The sound was very unfamiliar. It was the first time I had heard such crying. I turned and looked into the crib and it was the baby. I still did not think of her as my daughter; she was "the baby." She cried for a bit and I could not bring myself to pick her up. I wasn't sure what to do. I did the only thing I knew to do; I called the nurse. I pressed the button located near my bed and waited. As I waited, the baby's wailing became louder and sharper.

The nurse came in and headed straight for the crib. She looked inside the crib and asked why I hadn't picked up the baby. "I don't know what's wrong with her," I said. "Is she hungry, in pain?" "Well, she might be hungry. Are you going to breastfeed or bottle feed?" she asked again. I answered with the first response that came to my mind. "Bottle feed," I said without hesitation. "Okay, I'll prepare the bottle and you can feed her." She handed me the baby and the bottle, positioned her so she would be able to bottle feed and stayed while the baby latched on to it. "You are good to go" was all she said and left.

As I cradled this strange baby in my arms, feeding her, I looked at her in detail. She had fine, tender features. Her face was a pale white, but her cheeks were rosy. She had big brown eyes and a cute button nose. Her lips were perfectly formed and a bright pink. She was wearing a cap, a hospital cap with blue and pink stripes on it. I was afraid to take it off as I had a firm grip on her and the bottle. She took feeding seriously; I mean she was totally into the bottle. It must have taken about ten minutes for her to drink that small amount of milk and during the whole time I could not take my eyes off of her. I was amazed at this little person I was holding. The nurse came in and showed me how to burp her. All the parenting lessons I had taken at the teen parent program served me no good. I had forgotten everything.

The nurse checked her diaper for me and showed me how to "burrito" wrap her in her hospital blanket. She tucked her away in the crib and placed the crib next to my bed. I thought she was going to take the baby back to the nursery but she didn't. She left the baby in my room next to me. "Wait, aren't you taking the baby back to the nursery with you?" I asked. "Oh no," she said. "The baby stays with you in the room." "Could you take her back so I can sleep?" "No hun, the policy is that you keep her in your room." "Ugh." All I wanted to do was sleep and not have her in there. What if she cried again? What if something happened to her? I knew that in the nursery she would be safe and I would be able to sleep. I laid down again, facing her this time, and closed my eyes. Everything was just too overwhelming. Where was my mom, where was Jesse and my sisters were my last thoughts as I closed my eyes.

Once again I awoke to the crying of the baby. "What now? Is she not going to let me sleep?" I sat up and looked in the crib. I knew she was not hungry because she had just been fed. "What could be wrong this time?" I could not bring myself to pick her up even though moments earlier I had cradled her in my arms and fed her. I did the only thing I knew. I pressed the emergency button for the nurse again. A few minutes later the nurse was in my room. "Yes hun, what do you need?" she asked. "The baby is crying," was all I could mutter. "Well, did you check her diaper?" "No," I responded. "Okay, well, let's check her diaper."

The nurse uncovered her from her blankets, changed her diaper and expertly wrapped her up. She placed her back in the crib and left. It happened so fast and this time she must have been in a hurry because she did not take the time to explain how to change a diaper. I was not interested in listening to her explain how to change it either. I did not want to do anything. I slid back into my blankets and again she began to cry and again I called the nurse. "Now what is wrong?" This time her voice was not so sweet and kind. "She's crying again," I responded. "Honey, this is YOUR daughter and you have to learn to take care of her. You cannot keep calling me for everything. You will take her home and you will need to take care of her yourself. Now she ate already and she has already been changed. She probably needs to feel your warmth and lay with you. Take her and cuddle with her in the bed. She needs warmth!" Her firm voice almost made me cry. The nurse had just scolded me about my own baby. To top it off, she wanted me to lay with her.

Was she crazy? I wanted to sleep. I wanted to sleep forever, but that was not going to happen. I held this baby in my arms and laid her next to me. She stopped crying, but I did not sleep. I slid down into the bed, cradled her in my arms and cried. I did not sleep as I was afraid I would squish her to death. I had already killed a few baby chicks in my younger years by falling asleep and rolling over them in my bed. What if I did the same to her? I stayed up until Jesse arrived. He took over feeding her and changing her diaper. He was really happy. I could see it in his face. Proud to be a father. He did not have a problem feeding and changing diapers and cradling her. It was almost as if he knew her from the past. They had a bond, a bond that I did not have with her. I watched him and wondered why it was so hard for me. It made me feel better though to know that she had someone who loved her and cared for her.

I could not bring myself to love her just yet and that was hard for me. My mother and sisters came to visit. But the memories are vague. I was not in my full consciousness. The next day the nurse came in to ask about the name on the birth certificate. Jesse and I had already agreed that we would give her the feminine name of Jesse. So it would be Jessica. My older sister convinced me to give her a middle name. "There are a lot of Jessicas," she said. "You have to give her a name that will make her stand out." I thought for a moment and then agreed. I always respected my sister's advice. I looked up to her and felt that everything she said I had to follow. So we discussed a few middle names and came up with Vanessa. I would name her Jessica Vanessa Gomez. They stamped her feet on a certificate and wrote her name on it. "Wow! This little human being who had no name, no identity other than my daughter, now had a name of her own. A name that I had control giving her.

On the last day of my hospital stay, Jesse dressed her up in a beautiful strawberry outfit she had received for my baby shower a month before. I had a baby shower that I had not expected because my family was not into show-ing off the fact that I was expecting. So Jesse's aunt was kind enough to have one for me. I only had a friend or two and my mom and sisters went. It was mostly Jesse's family. They were all so kind in giving me gifts and wishing me well. That had been the only time that I felt a sense of being pregnant; the only time I had actually worn a maternity outfit. Before then it had been just baggy clothes. Clothes to hide the fact that I was a teen mom. I don't recall who gave her the outfit that we dressed her up in before she left the hospital but she looked precious. Perfectly precious.

Leaving the hospital was difficult. "How would I take care of this baby?" and what if I screwed this whole mother thing up. To begin with, I did not feel like a mother. My emotions were still numb. I did not feel excitement or joy at the thought of bringing my daughter home. Actually, I was terrified at the thought of having to take her to the apartment where not even I felt safe. "Would the neighbors be drinking next door? Would gang members roam the parking lot? I hated the thought of going back there, but we had no choice. That was our home. Nothing was as I had planned.

The apartment complex was quiet; it was still too early for people to be out and about. As we entered the apartment, I was struck by how we did not have anything ready. To begin with, we didn't have a lot of furniture, maybe a sofa. The kitchen came with the necessities of a stove and refrigerator and we had a few dishes but that's it. I walked into the bedroom followed by Jesse carrying the car seat with our newborn inside. He placed the car seat next to the bed where I sat. I was tired so I immediately sat down on the bed. I realized that Jessica's crib was just as I had left it — undone. The crib had already been given to me assembled. It had been assembled at the baby shower and was used to place the gifts inside. When I saw that I thought it was a wonderful idea. I loved seeing all the gifts neatly placed inside the crib. When I unwrapped the gifts I placed them back in the crib. Someone had washed some of the baby's clothes and neatly folded it. Pink and white tiny socks, pink and white body suits with little buttons the size of my fingernails clipped at the bottom as access to be able to change her diaper. A few tiny dresses, towels, wipes, diapers and baby jumpsuits.

As I looked at the crib I could not bring myself to organize any of it. "What was wrong with me?" This should have been the happiest time of my life. I had wanted this baby; I wanted a family to belong to and now I did not feel part of any of it. I was sad. Jesse must have seen the look on my face, the empty look. He quickly jumped into action and assembled the bedding in the crib. All I could do was stare. "How does it look?" he asked. "Good" I replied. The baby was still asleep when he picked her up and placed her in the newly decorated crib. She looked peaceful and beautiful.

I settled in and put away some of the stuff that I had brought home from the hospital: milk bottles, diapers and my clothes. I made sure to put her baby bottles away in a place where the cockroaches wouldn't get to them. In this apartment, I had no control over the amount of roaches that invaded us each day and night. I did my best to buy different traps and poisons to kill them but no luck. Every day and every night they were there. I took a shower and went to bed. I laid down and after a few minutes Jesse came in to say he had to run some errands. "Oh no!" was my first reaction. "You mean you're leaving me with the baby alone?" My voice breaking as if I was about to start bawling. Not sure if I wanted to cry or it was due to fear. Maybe both. "You'll be fine. I will come back shortly. Call me if anything and lock the door." I got up to lock the door behind him and went to bed again. "Please Lord, don't let her wake up until Jesse gets home." was all I could say.

I walked back into the bedroom and stood by Jessica's crib and stared. I watched her sleep for a moment and then trepidation set in. I began getting scared that she would die. "What if she turns around and suffocates herself? What if she stops breathing?" I calmed myself down enough to assure myself that nothing would happen to her. I laid down and turned to face the wall. As much as I did not want to see anything, I had a view out the window. Being on the second floor of the apartment building was a good thing. I could open my window and stare into the sky. I did not have to worry about people passing by or breaking in. I felt somewhat safe.

I must have fallen asleep for some time when Jessica's whimpering woke me up. I was not sure what to do. Although I was seventeen, common sense maturity or motherly instinct hadn't blossomed quite just yet. I thought for a second and decided that the best thing to do was call my mother. "She will know what I should do."

I dialed my mom's number and waited anxiously for her to answer. Each ring felt like minutes as my daughter's wailing got louder. In her Spanish she answered, "Hello." "Mom, it's me." "What's wrong?" she asked. "Well, the baby is crying in the crib and I am not sure what to do." "Alicia, she must be hungry. Babies eat every three hours you know." Somehow I had forgotten that part. Or maybe I had not been paying attention to my parenting classes as well as I should have. Every three hours seemed like a lot.

"Do you still have the hospital bottles of milk they gave you?" she asked. "Yes, I responded." "Use those until you get the WIC formula." WIC was the government assistance program that provided baby formula and food for me. Every month I had to go into the office, listen to some nutrition classes, answer some questions and provide evidence that I was on low income; otherwise, I wouldn't qualify. In return they would give me vouchers to purchase baby formula, milk, cereal, eggs and other staple foods. I had not been given the baby formula just yet, but thankfully the hospital gave me enough pre-made bottles to last me until the week's appointment. "Okay, I am going to open a bottle and give it to her," I replied. "Call me if you need me again," she said. Yeah, she should be here helping me I thought, but I did not say it. "Okay," was all that I said.

I hung up the phone and opened the bottle. I picked Jessica out of her crib and tried to find a good position for me to feed her. It did not come naturally like the way you see other mothers do it, or the way they show it on TV. She took to the bottle right away and drank to her heart's content. When she finished, I remembered to burp her. I had made that mistake at the hospital and the nurse yelled at me when Jessica developed gas. I did not hold her too long. I still had issues holding her. I put her back in her crib, sat down on the bed, and cried. I was not sure why I was crying, but the tears flowed incessantly and the sadness in my heart would not go away.

I had not been crying for too long when Jessica started to cry again. I had just fed her and burped her and she was crying again. I called my mother. "Alicia, check her diaper, she might need to be changed," she said. Wow, now that was a thought. Change the baby's diaper. I was starting to wonder if I learned anything in the parenting classes. I picked Jessica up again and smelled her butt first. I had seen some mothers do that before, I figured it would work for me and I wouldn't have to unbutton her jumpsuit and actually see the poop or pee. It worked, she smelled. "Okay, now how do I do this again?" I picked up a diaper and analyzed it closely before I began the process of unbuttoning her jumpsuit and removing the poopy diaper. I don't know exactly if I was staring at the diaper hoping Jesse would return at that moment and take over. He had been the one changing most of her diapers in the hospital. Or maybe I was waiting for Jessica to change her own diaper. It took me a while to build the courage to do it. It was not because I was grossed out about changing a diaper, I simply felt inadequate thinking I would do it wrong.

"Here goes nothing," I thought. I placed her on the bed, unbuttoned her jumpsuit and undid her diaper. "OMG, what is that?" What I saw in her diaper changed my mind about changing it. How would I clean up that mess? It would take a whole box of wipes to clean that up. "Maybe I should just place her in the bathtub and wash her that way," one of many thoughts. "No, I have to do this." I slowly began the steps of changing a soiled diaper. I wiped and wiped and wiped. I must have given her a wipe rash from wiping so much. I proceeded to switch the dirty diaper with the clean one and then tape it on the sides. Success! Jessica made no noise as she was being changed. I think she knew she would stress me out more if she cried. She was born smart. As I began to button her jumpsuit back up my worst fear came to light. "I did not do this right!" I had skipped a step. I had forgotten to put baby powder on her butt to avoid a rash. I felt horrible, but not enough to redo it. I figured Jesse would have to change her diaper again soon. I would remind him to sprinkle her with baby powder. A few hours without the powder would not kill her.

Once the changing diaper process was all done, I looked at Jessica., She seemed happy, so I put her back in her crib. I was done, or so I thought. She started crying again. I had done everything my mother said I should do. This was just unbelievable. I had to call someone again. I debated whether to call my mom or Jesse this time. If I called Jesse, he would think I did not know what I was doing and I felt bad about that. If I called my mom again, she would probably lecture me just like the nurse did. Her lecture, however, would be in more detail and more stern. Honestly, I did not want to hear it. I debated and eventually, I took the chance and called my mother yet again. I did not even bother saying hello. "She's crying again and I changed her diaper and fed her. What's wrong with her?" I asked. She lectured me in Spanish. Lectures in Spanish sounded more harsh than in English, just like the curse words. "Alicia, this is your child," she pointed out. "You need to take care of her and know what she wants. If you don't, then you need to guess. It could only be one of a few things; she's hungry, she has a dirty diaper, she has gas or she needs your warmth. And you already took care of all the above except for cradling her. You need to cradle her in your arms and lay her down with you for warmth," was her answer. There we go again. Did she not know that I was tired? I did not say anything other than, "Okay, I will cradle her."

I hung up the phone, picked up Jessica and laid her down next to me in the bed. She was wrapped in her blanket, burrito style. That I had been able to do. Not the best burrito because her dad did a much better job at wrapping her up, but she was wrapped. I held her in my arms. She stopped crying and closed her eyes. I wanted so much to close mine, but the fear of squishing her was too much for me to bear. I was not going to be able to sleep thinking that as tired as I was I feared suffocating her to death. So I laid there, eyes wide open, tears rolling down my face. It was my first day with my daughter at home.

Chapter 20

Teen Mom

I began to slowly adjust to holding Jessica and feeding her, yet my hope that her father would take over all the time remained. I often packed her things and drove over to my mom's house to visit. At the time she had her hands full taking care of my nephew, but overall she would take care of my daughter as well. She would feed her and carry her. As soon as I knew her dad would be home, I would pack up, get into the small, burgundy four-door Datsun my mom had given me, and I would drive us back to the apartments.

As I began to approach the apartments I would get a sick feeling in my stomach. I hated living there. I hated the men who would just stand around gawking, that gave me the creeps. Their drinking made it worse. Nonetheless, I had to get back, it was after all our home.

Three weeks into us living there my emotions began a spiral downward. I began to cry over everything and anything. I was sad and confused with this whole parenting thing and now add to that the bills and adult responsibilities Jesse and I had to deal with. It was overwhelming.

We began to argue and the verbal arguments became increasingly worse. I was very unhappy. I was miserable and I missed living with my mom immensely. When Jessica was about a month old, my mom came over to visit and I was in a really bad shape. I had not showered in days and I laid in bed mostly. We sat on my bed as she carried the baby and asked how I was doing. I think that must have been the first time she had asked since Jessica had been born. I did not mind because I knew she had her hands full taking care of my one-year old nephew. I was also glad she had not asked before because I would have probably said "fine," and the conversation would have ended and she would not have asked me for another month. But I was not fine.

I had not been fine since Jessica's birth and it was getting worse. Her timing was perfect because I was at my lowest point and that opened me up to answering her truthfully. I stood up because I felt as if my chest was going to burst and my tears would flow. I had to stand up and not let her see me cry. I was prepared to say "Fine," but as I stood next to the bedroom window looking out, something below caught my attention. A man was inside his car looking up at me staring out the window. An old man probably in his fifties. He had parked his car right underneath the window and moved over to the passenger side. I stood there trying to figure out what he was trying to do. He scooted himself over to the passenger side and began to make inappropriate gestures at me and gawk. I did not need this now. This was the last thing I needed, a pervert making things worse. I could not go any worse emotionally.

I broke into that gushing waterfall of tears and ran into the bathroom. My mother, still carrying my daughter, ran behind me. *"Que te pasa, Alicia?"* "What's wrong, Alicia?" How could I begin to tell her what was wrong? How could I tell her that I was questioning my decision to be a parent. How could I say, "Maybe I am just not cut out to be a mother. I don't know how to be one. I don't feel anything for my daughter. I hate this place and I hate living with Jesse. I JUST WANT TO GO BACK HOME."

I was able to utter the last few things, I hated living with Jesse and I wanted to go home. I also told her about the man below. But, by the time she went to check, he was gone. I came out of the bathroom and sat on the bed next to her. She saw how desperate and sad I was that she suggested I move out right away. The only problem was that moving back home was not an option. My step dad still could not accept Jesse and my mom felt that we needed to continue trying to work on being parents. She called my sisters to ask for suggestions and Veronica suggested we move into the one-bedroom apartment below hers. The apartment had been recently vacated. My sister had been living there for a while with her husband and her five-year old son.

I took her up on her offer and moved out of the apartment and into the small 500 square foot apartment below hers. By then we had a living room set and two sofas that would only fit facing each other. This left a small walkway to the bedroom and bathroom and up to the kitchen.

It was a tiny house. We had a bedroom set that consisted of a bed and a dresser that did not match. Jessica had her own dresser that was different from the other ones. Somehow, we made a bedroom set out of pieces of furniture we found. We did not have money to fix up the place nicely, so we used what we had available to us. We used bed sheets as curtains for both the living room windows and the bedroom windows. It was not very nice, but it was a home and the most important thing was making sure that Jessica's crib fit. Now I was living with Jesse and my daughter a few steps from my sister's apartment. I felt a sense of comfort knowing that if I needed her, she would be there. Jesse was working for a pizza place making and delivering pizzas. He was not making much money, and what he earned he spent on fixing up his car.

I decided to re-enroll in my high school. It was my senior year and I wanted to make sure I graduated on time and with my class: Mtn. View High School 1994. My sister offered to watch my daughter while I was at school, which made it very easy and comforting. I was secure and at peace knowing that she would be well taken care. On days Jesse would go to work late, he would stay with her and then drop her off with my sister. My first day back to school was difficult. I had not set foot back at my high school since I had left to finish my junior year at a teen parenting school. The drive to school killed me. I had to drive from East Los Angeles to El Monte every day and since I am not a morning person, I would always end up running late. I took the freeway and tried not to get caught speeding. It was not the safest thing to do, but at the time I did not realize the importance of not speeding. To me not getting detention for being tardy was more important.

Only a few people knew the reason why I had left, so the first day back was filled with many questions by people who knew me. I had my schedule of classes already. Shortly after my daughter was born in August, I went to my high school to get the classes I needed to graduate. My schedule was odd. I had three classes that I needed to graduate and three classes that I did not need. I had something like art, drama, and typing. I did not need the classes because I had all the credits that I needed to graduate, but according to the law I had to be in school for a set number of hours.

That first day, as I entered each class, it felt very different. My friends had made new friends; everyone had their own groups they would hang out with while I had been gone. I could not relate to anything that they would talk about and many times I felt left out. More than before. They would make plans to go out after school or talk about upcoming dances and games and nothing they spoke about I could get involved with. My days of being a teenager were over. They had never really started and somehow they were already over. I could not go to dances or movies after school. I could not just "hang out" at someone's house or wherever. I could no longer watch football games and stay out until late at night, not that I ever did. Now that I was older I could not do it because I had to go straight home to stay with my daughter.

I recall my typing class; advanced typing because I had already taken typing 1 during my sophomore year. My teacher was the same teacher I had had before. As I entered his class, he greeted me with great enthusiasm and asked where I had been. Just like I had said to everyone else, I explained to him the story of why I chose to leave the school. I told him about my daughter and as I did, I remember seeing this expression on his face that made me wonder what he was thinking. Before I could ask, he shared his thoughts, "Elva, I can tell you are a mother," he said. "Something about a woman changes when she becomes a mother, I think it's your skin" he said. "My skin?" Hmmm. I could have guessed the dark circles under my eyes and the bulgy left over tummy that I could not get rid of were the giveaways for me. How would my skin change? I did not want him to explain as I did not want to add "skin changing" to my list of things that had changed in my life since becoming a mother.

Since Jessica was born, she would wake up every three or four hours at night to eat. Jesse and I had an understanding that we would take turns waking up to feed her. Every other day was my day and we would trade weekends sometimes. One weekend I would do the night feedings and the following weekend was his. The bottles were prepared ahead of time with the concentrated milk already inside each bottle and I made enough to cover the day and night feedings. We had several bottles in the refrigerator ready with the milk and just waiting for us to pour the warm water in them.

The nights that I had to get up were miserable. I loved to sleep so anytime my sleep was taken from me it felt like torture, especially around her 1 am and 5 am feedings. I felt as if I had just entered the most beautiful part of my deep sleep when her crying would wake me up. Several times at night I would elbow Jesse and tell him those were his nights to get up, knowing quite well I was lying. He would fall for them often, other times he would stay quiet and think for a few seconds and then he would remember what day of the week it was and remind me it was really my turn. I would act surprised and say, "oh yeah, you're right." I would hesitantly get up and get a bottle for her. I hate to admit it because it makes me feel like a bad mother, but there were times, not many though, that I was half asleep and I would forget to add water to the bottle of concentrated milk. I would just warm it up as it was, with concentrated milk. I would then pick her up from her crib, feed her, burp her and put her back in her crib. Jessica never complained. I realized what I had been doing after I washed a few of her bottles only to smell the strong smell of concentrated milk. She never got sick enough for me to take her to the doctor, but I did notice her being constipated a few times.

Once I realized my mistake, I began paying more attention to how I prepared her bottles. I would go back to bed, only to be woken up by one of two things, Jessica crying or mice traveling up and down the bed through our sheets. At the other apartment, I had to deal with cockroaches, in this apartment, I had to deal with mice. It took Jesse and me a while to figure out what was waking us up on days that Jessica was fast asleep. One day when I was in a light sleep I felt something moving in between the sheets. As I picked it up I saw this little creature scurry down the foot of the bed. I screamed as loud as I could and jumped out of bed. "What's wrong, what's the matter?" yelled Jesse. I could tell he was not fully awake, but his flight or fight response had kicked in and he was trying to make sense of what was going on. "There's a mouse on the bed and I think it's what wakes us up at night." We got up, turned on the light and searched all around the bed. We confirmed it was a mouse because right below our headboard was a small hole in the wall. It had jagged edges from where the mouse or mice had gnawed at and there were mice droppings on the floor.

I cried. I cried out of being tired, I cried out of frustration, disgust, sadness. "How can I have my daughter live in a mouse infested home? Have these mice been in her crib with her?" I must have cried all night alone in the living room while Jesse and Jessica were asleep in the bedroom.

My routine of coming and going to and from school continued for a few weeks. In those weeks I ended up with several detention slips for being tardy. I just couldn't get ready in time to leave my house and drive several miles to school every day. I was not disciplined enough to get myself up early and leave early enough. Not to mention, school just was not the same. It all seemed so superficial. I was not a normal teenager anymore and most of my friends were there to spend their senior year experiencing what seniors do: dances, friends, proms and rallies. Not that there was anything wrong with that, I just was not into that. My mind was on raising a child, cleaning my home and paying bills.

I continued receiving government assistance, also known at the time as Welfare and Food Stamps. I would get a check for money that would help with costs for me and my daughter. I would also get these funny looking coupons that resembled money called Food Stamps. I could spend the money however way I wanted, but the Food Stamps needed to be used for food. I had grown up with food stamps because my mother received both as well. I also knew that it was a shameful thing to get. People often looked down upon people receiving government assistance. It was like getting charity because we were poor. My older sister taught me that. She was always embarrassed to go to the grocery store with food stamps. "Why can't you give me money instead of food stamps?" she would ask my mom. My mom did not care. To her, money was money. I, however, grew up with the feeling that food stamps were shameful. Nonetheless, I used them. We needed them.

Jesse would help with some money, but most of the financial responsibility fell on me. I had to pay the rent and pay the bills. Oftentimes, we argued because he would rather spend his pizza earnings on fixing up his car with nice rims and nice stereos instead of helping to buy better furniture or decent curtains. He was out a lot as well. Spending time with his friends had become more important than being at home with us. So when I got out of school, I would pick up my daughter from my sister's house and walk down the stairs to my house. Many times my sister would ask to keep Jessica longer. My nephew would still be at school and my sister's husband would be at work so she did not mind keeping my daughter longer. I did not mind either.

I still had not fully bonded with Jessica. It was still difficult for me to show affection toward her. It didn't feel natural to hug and kiss her and sing songs to her like a real mother would do. At four months all she wanted was to be fed, changed and picked up once in a while. During the times that my sister would keep her longer I would get home and start my homework. I was tired most of the time, tired from lack of sleep and tired of having the responsibility of keeping a home in order. I was tired of thinking about all I needed to do and tired of being sad. I was tired of being tired all the time. And I still had homework to complete.

On days that my sister could not keep Jessica longer, I would feed her and hope she would fall asleep in order for me to get my work done. I knew I could not count on Jesse to help me because I never knew when he would be home. Most days Jessica would fall asleep, but on the days that she wouldn't, I would place her in her car seat on the floor and with one foot I would rock her back and forth while I read or worked on my writing assignments.

Jessica was a quiet and happy baby as long as she was fed and her diaper was clean. Rocking her back and forth in her car seat while I did homework was fun for her. There were times, however, when she would cry and cry. I never knew if she was just having a bad day or just needed a longer nap. Regardless, I tried as best as I could to console her. I would hold her and rock her and if that didn't work, I would just leave her in her crib and close the bedroom door behind me. It was difficult not knowing what she wanted and not being able to comfort her. Sometimes my frustration would set in after listening to her cry for a long time. From the living room I would yell at her to be quiet. Sometimes it would go further and tell her to "shut up already," all the while covering my ears.

My ability to deal with her needs was very limited. I was still trying to deal with all the other responsibilities I had of being an adult and yet not really an adult. The stress of everything I had to deal with began to take its toll. The depression became worse and the feeling of inadequacy with my daughter was also greater. Still, I would hold her when necessary. There were times though that I did feel "it"; when I fed her or bathed her, I sensed the love that was somehow buried. I knew I loved her because the thought of anything bad happening to her made me cringe. I made sure all her needs were met and many times I would go into the room to check on her. I wanted to make sure she was still breathing and okay.

Chapter 21

The Abuse

Verbal fights between Jesse and me became frequent. The demands of being parents and trying to cope with growing up ourselves were tough. We would fight almost every day. Jessica was about eleven months old now and was keen to know what was going on. Jesse and I would fight about money and who would take care of Jessica. He wanted to spend all his money on his car. All the while, we did not have good furniture or curtains on the windows. I was on government assistance and not much was left over for clothing and other necessities. I was lucky enough that my older sister would give me a lot of her hand-me downs from her son. He was a year older, so she would give me all the clothes that no longer fit him. It was a regular sight to see Jessica wearing sweat pants, sweatshirts and T-shirts with dinosaurs or car designs on them. I had a blue and green warm blanket with dinosaurs on it that we loved to wrap her in as well. Jesse and I also fought about how much time he spent out with his friends. I did not have the luxury to be out with friends, so I figured he too should be home with his family. Usually, after his shift at the pizza place was over, he would not come home.

On one occasion, when he did come home, we had a fight. Many times it began as an ordinary conversation that would escalate to yelling. This day it went further. We began arguing about how much time he spent with his friends when he decided to leave. I watched him leave the house and figured he had left for the day. Since Jessica was asleep I decided to take a shower.

As I turned the water on I heard the front door open. He had come back and he was infuriated. He was yelling at me as he came through the door and pushed the bathroom door open. I turned to look at him and did not have time to react when the first punch to my face came. All I saw was a fist flying across the small bathroom space and straight to my face. I did not feel the pain initially. I must have blacked out for a second because I don't remember if he punched me a second time. The next thing I knew I was crying in the bathroom shower holding my jaw while cold water was running down my shaking body. I was in immense pain.

After a few minutes under the running water, still holding my jaw I dried myself and sat in the living room and cried some more. I was in complete and utter shock. After months of not experiencing physical violence it had returned. Late that night I went to bed after taking some Tylenol to ease the pain. It reduced the pain a little, but I knew something was wrong with my jaw. I could not open or close my mouth properly without pain, and it was not opening all the way. I felt that my jaw had been dislocated. Jessica had slept through the whole event and later woke up to eat. I pretended as if nothing happened and continued with my mommy responsibilities. I was thankful that she had not seen or heard anything.

The next day, I left my daughter with my sister and instead of going to school, I went straight to see a doctor. As I sat there I began to think of a story to tell so the doctor would not know that I had been beaten. I could not say that. I was ashamed and embarrassed and worried that something terrible would happen to Jesse because of what he did to me. I could not come up with a story fast enough when I was called to the counter. "Elva, why are you seeing the doctor today?" the receptionist asked. "My jaw hurts because I was in a car accident." I was surprised at how fast I was able to come up with a story once I had been asked. "Okay, have a seat and the nurse will call you in a minute." I said thank you and sat down.

Now that I had a story, I had a few minutes to come up with the details and make it believable. I began telling the story to myself in order to practice perfecting it. "I was driving with my friend Claudia and we hit a car and I hit the dashboard because I was not wearing my seatbelt." Yup this would be the details I would stick with. It was an easy story and no one would get hurt. "Elva please come on in," called the nurse. It was time for me to sound confident to tell my story to the nurse and the doctor. I was nervous and hoped that they would not ask me anything further. The nurse came in and took my vitals. She asked me again why I was there and I told her my car accident story. She seemed to believe it, I was safe. Then the doctor came in and asked me the same question. "Elva, why are you here today." By this time I had told my story twice so it became easier to lie.

"I am sorry to hear that you had an accident, let's take a few x-rays and see what's going on." Off I went to the x-ray machine. Once the x-rays were taken and the doctor had read them he came back into the room to give me his diagnosis. I was sitting on the examination table, waiting anxiously for the results. I was still in pain and the Tylenol I had taken earlier was starting to wear off. He confirmed what I had suspected. "Elva, looks like your jaw is dislocated. It is not broken so that's a good thing. I need to move your jaw a little and it's going to hurt." With a few moves to my jaw and a lot of pain, he repositioned my jaw. "You should still feel pain for a while so continue taking Tylenol. You should feel better in a few days."

I went home and rested and after a few hours picked up my daughter from my sister's house. Jesse hardly spent time at home. He would look for any excuse to go out after work. I would spend my time with my daughter doing mommy duties.

This time allowed Jessica and me to bond a little. Jessica was about eight months and I watched her say her first word and go from crawling to taking a few first steps. She remained a happy baby so that was great to see. I don't think any of Jesse and my issues affected her. As for the mouse, I covered that hole and never again did I see one. I began to feel more comfortable with the role of being a mommy. I had overcome the idea that I would not be a normal teenager.

My relationship with Jesse continued to deteriorate. We could not get along and when he was home we were always arguing. One night at about one in the morning I received a phone call from the El Monte Police. "Hello, this is the El Monte Police." I was half asleep, but when I heard those words my body quickly went into flight or fight response. My eyes opened wide and my senses became very keen. I knew it was serious. "We have a Jesse in the back of our police car. He was involved in a vehicle accident and he needs someone to pick him up." I could not process what he was saying. All I heard was "accident, Jesse and pick him up." They gave me the location and I quickly grabbed Jessica from her crib, strapped into her car seat and took off. As I drove all I could think of was if he was okay. Jessica slept the whole time.

When I arrived, I saw a lonely street blocked off with yellow tape. I parked behind one police car and got off. A police officer approached me and asked if I was there to pick up Jesse and I said yes. "Follow me," he said. As he led me to another cop car, he explained that Jesse had collided with another car and unfortunately the other driver did not survive the crash. I looked at the wreckage and the yellow sheet covering the body inside the other car. Both cars were severely damaged. It looked as if he had crashed into a wall. The whole front of the car was a total wreck.

How he survived that accident was a miracle. I felt that what I saw should have had two deaths and not one. But, it was not Jesse's time to die. The police officer led me to where Jesse was, in the back of a police car. "Jesse is not going to be charged. It was an accident and the other driver was probably drunk since he slammed into Jesse's car. You can take him home." I ran to the back of the car and as soon as he came out of the car I gave him a hug and asked if he was okay. He did not have a scratch on him.

We drove home that night, thankful he was not injured. As for his car, I had mixed feelings. I was sad to see it smashed but happy that it was gone. He had been celebrating having finished fixing the car exactly the way he wanted it that night. It had nice tires and rims and had just spent money on an expensive stereo and seat covers. The money that was meant for our curtains had gone into that car. It felt like Karma kicking in. Karma waited until he had finished the car to take it away from him. We drove home in silence and went to bed.

I was exhausted and had to wake up early to feed Jessica and go to school the next day. A few hours later I awoke to Jessica crying. I fed her, put her back in her crib and got ready for school. As I was driving to school, many thoughts rushed to my head. The man who had died in the crash the night before made it clear life was short and not guaranteed.

I was not feeling high school anymore. It wasn't my environment. I had matured as a mother and had different interests from my friends. Things they said or did seemed superficial to me. I wasn't happy that I had to spend so many hours at school taking useless classes like wood shop just to fill the requirements of the law.

On the drive to school, I decided that I would take myself out of my school and enroll at the local adult school to finish my classes. When I got to school, I went straight to the office and let them know that I needed to enroll in the adult school because I had babysitting issues. They gave me the paperwork and I was out of there in less than an hour. I went home to find Jesse up already. We sat on the sofa and talked about what had happened the night before. He explained that he was driving to his friend's house when the car behind him ran into him, causing both of them to spin out of control. Jesse's car hit the fence near some buildings a few times, while the man's car flipped over. The man was not wearing his seatbelt which caused him to break through the windshield, fall to the street and die. I was horrified at the thought of what had happened. I was also saddened to hear about the man dying. Jesse was pretty upset that the accident happened the day he was celebrating, having completed all the work on his car. "Why are you here so early from school?" He asked. I explained I would no longer be going to high school because I wanted to spend more time with my daughter. At that point, I was bonding with my daughter more. It was still difficult, but it was becoming normal for me. We had a routine, and I was getting to know her.

The following week I began my classes at the adult school. I would have a minimum of three hours a day to complete work in a few academic areas. Three hours a day did not seem so bad and it was all independent work. I would go into a large classroom setting at any time of the day and work quietly. I would read the chapters in the book and complete the worksheets that came with them. Once completed I would turn them in for credit. My goal was to finish high school as planned, along with the rest of the 1994 graduating class. I did not intend to walk at the graduation with my class. It was acceptable for me to receive my diploma at the adult school and go home to be with my daughter.

Jesse was not thrilled about the idea of me going to the adult school. Not sure why. On several occasions he had gone to my school and pulled me out of class only to insult me and call me names in the hallway of the school. Twice

I had to endure physical abuse during school hours. Once I was in the middle of studying in the classroom when he entered the room and asked me to go outside. I was embarrassed and scared at the same time. I walked out into the hallway to meet with him. He pinned me to the wall and with his face right in front of mine he began to belittle me and insult me. I could feel the breath of his anger on my face and because I did not want to make a scene I stayed quiet.

At that point, people began to walk by, so I began walking to the parking lot. Somehow I made it to his car so that we could talk in private. I thought we would "talk" but the truth was that he simply wanted to insult and belittle me. His friend had been sitting in the back seat so I figured things would not get out of hand. But Jesse wanted to appear powerful in front of his friend that not only did he insult and yell at me, but he went as far as punching me. This time his fist made it to my cheek. I felt the raw burn of his fist hitting my face. I did not feel pain immediately. All I could hear was his friend telling him to stop. I managed to get out of the car and while doing so he hit me with the door of the car. Somehow he had flung the door open and it struck me in the stomach removing all air from my lungs. As soon as I was able to catch my breath I began running back to school.

He did not follow me as I went back inside. I went straight to the bathroom and washed my face from traces of crying. I checked for any bruises but all I had was some redness on my cheeks. Once I gathered myself together, I went back into my classroom and tried to finish my work. I was able to disconnect myself from what had just happened with my school work. It gave me an escape from reality. After the three hours at school, it was time for me to go home. I managed to pick up my daughter and go home. I had a feeling that Jesse would not show up that night and I was right.

After I had put Jessica to bed, I went into the bathroom to wash my face. As I looked at my reflection, I thought about how I had let the situation get this bad. I didn't have an answer. I could not figure out what I had done to deserve the abuse I was getting. I stared at myself for a while and began to cry. I cried and cried. I sat in the corner of the bathroom hoping that it would all end. I looked at my hands and the thought of suicide came to me again. I pictured myself taking a razor blade and slashing my wrists. I imagined the blood slowly running out of my veins as I took my last few breaths. "Maybe this time it would succeed." I was tired and sad. With all these dark thoughts, love brought me back to my senses. I thought about my daughter and how she would grow up without a mother. I thought about missing to see her grow up. I thought about my family and how devastated they would be.

Once again I made myself believe that all this suffering would disappear soon. All the bad things would end if I could just hang in there another day. I mustered what little strength I had, got up, wiped my tears and headed to bed. I laid my head on the pillow, hoping to fall into one of my beautiful dreams that I had dreamt as a child. I prayed that my nightmares would not come back. I went to bed that night with love in my heart, love for my daughter who was now fast asleep in her crib.

Chapter 22

Taking the Bus

Jesse and I hardly saw each other as he rarely came home, and I was spending more and more time with my mom. After I got out of adult school I would pick up my daughter at my sister's and drive to my mom's house. Those drives were rough because my car did not have an air conditioner or heater. On cold days my daughter and I were really cold and on hot days we were hot inside the car. On hot days I drove with the windows down and the hot air would blow in our faces. Jessica, as sweaty as she was in her car seat, never once fussed at the scorching temperature. I told myself that when I had money, I would buy a car that had an air conditioner and a heater. I did not care about a nice stereo or anything else, I just didn't want to see her suffer in the winter cold or in the unbearable summer heat.

Once, after I got out of school, Jesse and I got into a fight, he took my car keys and left in my car. After the accident, it took him a while to get another car, so he would use mine periodically. I decided that even though he had taken my car, I would not stay home. I packed my daughter's stuff in her diaper bag, got her stroller, took some money and off I went to the bus stop. I was not about to allow anyone to stop me from going to school and going to my mom's house. Those were the only two places I felt at peace.

I walked about a mile to the bus stop. It was a long and arduous walk. How I managed to get to the bus stop with all that stuff and an eleven-month old on my arm I will never know. I waited a few minutes for the bus and as soon as I saw it coming I got up and grabbed my bag. I stood in line hoping that nothing would fall out of my hands. So far I had it juggled perfectly. I began to board the bus when I noticed that people were putting money in the money box. "Oh no!" I had forgotten, in my preoccupation to juggle everything in my hands, to take out money to pay for the darn bus. I did not even know how much it cost. It had been years since I rode on the bus.

As a child that was all I did with my mom; we were bus traveling experts. Since I had started driving, I no longer even noticed them. "I am sorry, I need to set the stuff down to get the money to pay you." I told the bus driver, very embarrassed. I felt like everyone was looking at me thinking, "She's holding up the bus." He looked at me and gave me a nod. It was not a nice nod.

He didn't wait for me to walk to a seat and there was only one seat available toward the back of the bus. "Lord, help me make it without falling, please." I was disappointed that no one on the bus got up to give up their seat. They had seen me carrying all this stuff, plus a baby. The bus driver did not care that I had to get to the end of the bus. He took off like a madman, and if you have ever been on a bus you know that trying to walk in there is a whole balancing act. Somehow I did not fall. I put all my stuff down wherever I could and sat down to take my money out of my bag. I managed to get the exact change, I did not care if it was more; I was not about to ask for change.

I got up again, holding a baby. I made it to the front to pay. Jessica had been quiet through the whole episode. I think she saw my frustration and decided to be calm and collected. She was a very mature baby.

I paid the bus driver and turned around to go back to my seat. I had Jessica on one arm so that I could hold onto the poles with the other hand and try to balance myself as this crazy bus driver rode the streets like a maniac. Unfortunately, I did not calculate my turn correctly because when I turned to grab onto one pole, Jessica's head hit the other one. I heard a loud "thump" and people turned to look at Jessica. Yup, I had hit her head on a pole. I looked at her to see if she was going to cry all the while thinking of my options if she did. I was not sure what a good mother should do. She did not cry, that strong child of mine. I went back to my seat and my tears began to roll down my eyes from the stress. It was part sadness that I had to go back to riding buses again and part out of happiness that I made it through the first part of

148

the bus ride to my mom's.

When I got to her house we had a heart to heart talk about my living situation. I did not tell her about the abuse as I was ashamed about it. I told her that I was unhappy and fighting with Jesse all the time. I told her he had taken the keys from me and that he would not spare money to buy necessities. I told her about the mice crawling in the bed and around the house and how I wanted to come home. That's all she needed to hear. "Come back home, I told you I would help you with this." I know she had wanted me to raise Jessica with Jesse but now that she saw that parenting was tough for me, she was agreeable with me going back home.

A month later I was back home. I was relieved to be back in my room and with my mom. I had left with a belly and had come back with a one-year old daughter. My stepfather was living with us and he did not seem to mind I was there. He just did not want Jesse over when he was there. That was the rule. He did not like Jesse at all.

Jesse and I continued to have a relationship; he would come to see Jessica and we would go out and eat. All that he had done to me was not enough for me to leave him completely. I loved him and it was hard to let go. Deep down inside, I still felt that perhaps at some future time we would live happily ever after, in a house with a white picket fence, just like in the fairy tales.

Now that I was home, I felt comfortable leaving my daughter to my mom. I would often lock myself in my room and Jessica would knock and I would not open. I was usually listening to music or reading and I did not want to be disturbed. I once again forgot that I was a mother and that I no longer had any privacy rights. During my moments of forgetfulness, my mom would come and practically tear down the door with her knocking. "You are not supposed to have this door closed and you are to let your daughter enter the room whenever she wants to." She would yell. Jessica would come in for a while and we would play; she would then leave to drink her bottle with grandma. I was back to feeling my age.

Since Jesse no longer had a car he was not able to pay me those horrible visits. I studied with peace and calm. I focused on what I needed to do and accomplished every last thing. School for me was a comfort.

In early May I was notified that I could graduate with my high school class. I was very excited. I wanted to walk down the aisle and get my diploma with all the people I knew from junior high school. However, after thinking about it for a long time, I decided that it would not be a wise decision. I remembered how I had felt being at school as a mother. I was no longer part of that group, the teenage group. Being surrounded by people I no longer knew and who did not know me would be difficult. Friends would congratulate each other and invite each other to their parties and I would be left out. I did not need that. I decided to just receive my diploma at the adult school.

In June, the same day my class of 1994 walked down the aisle in the graduation ceremony to receive their diplomas. I, Elva Alicia Leon, received mine in the tiny office of the counselor, someone I had only briefly met twice. "Congratulations Elva, here is your high school diploma." She shook my hand, I thanked her and went home.

I felt a great sense of accomplishment walking to my car. I had a piece of paper that I did not imagine I would have. My plans had changed, but not by much. I still had my goals and my dreams. I would go to college and get my bachelors and get a job. I wanted to be a social worker. I wanted to work with children who were in foster homes. I wanted to be the one who cared for them and let them know it would all be okay when they went to their court meetings. That's what I wanted to be.

I did not know that the road ahead of me would change many times and bring me more obstacles and challenges that would test my faith, my strength and my love for myself and others.

Chapter 23

Another Try

That summer was a beautiful summer. I enrolled at East Los Angeles College. It would be a drive from my house to the school. East LA College felt right. I spent that time applying for everything I could. I applied for financial aid and college aid. I was given so much money that it astonished me. Because I was a single parent, I received four thousand dollars that year plus all my classes, books and parking were paid for. I even received money for gas and child care. They paid my mom for watching Jessica.

That summer I got a job working for a supermarket. They had opened a market at the corner of my house and it was huge. I applied for and got the position of cashier. I trained for it and loved it. I worked mornings and was off in the afternoon so I would go home to help my mom take care of Jessica. I say help because my mom mostly did the job. By the time I got home, Jessica was bathed and had eaten. I would just play with her. My bond with her was growing stronger. Watching her play and laugh gave me a lot of joy. I was in awe of my daughter. I still could not believe that this beautiful thing had come from me. Still it was difficult to fathom that I was her mother. When I took her out with me to the store or to school to turn in papers, people would always say, "Oh, your sister is so cute." I did not get asked if she was mine. They automatically assumed she was my sister.

Part of me was fine with it and part of me wanted people to know that I was her mother. I did not want to be called her sister even though I was starting to feel that way. Jessica was calling my mom "Mom" and she would hear my nephew and my mom call me "Alicia" so she began calling me "Alicia." For some odd reason I never corrected her. There were times, however, when she would call me "Mami" Mommy in Spanish. The times she would say it seemed strange to me. It felt weird.

Being a cashier, allowed me the time to spend the evenings with Jessica. I felt more like a big sister playing with her little sister. Jessica would go to my mom for everything. When I tried to intervene or set rules and boundaries, my mother would not allow it. Pretty much what I said would not happen. As much as I hated it, I did not fight it. I could not win with my mom.

A few months after I began working at the supermarket, I started classes at East Los Angeles College. I was the second fastest cashier, so they gave me long hours even though I had asked for part time. My new schedule was full time classes in the morning, drive home, eat lunch and play with my daughter for an hour, change into my uniform for work, and leave. I would go to work at one in the afternoon and come home by nine. I suffered through this for many months.

Much as I loved work I hated having to leave my daughter all day. I only saw her for one hour a day. When I came home, she would be asleep. I tried to make up for my absence by buying her everything I could. I was no longer receiving government aid since my job paid pretty well at the time. I was making nine dollars an hour and my community college was giving me lots of money and perks.

Jessica had many toys and clothes that were no longer hand me downs from my nephew. I was tired dressing my daughter in dinosaur clothing. Because she was almost bald until she was one, people often thought she was a boy. I didn't like it. So now that I had money and she had a little bit of hair, I bought her dresses and girl overalls. Our yard had tons of toys. Jessica had a playhouse and swing set. She had a red push car and eventually she graduated to an electric Barbie car. She drove that thing around like it was no one's business. But that did not take away the fact that I still missed seeing her more often. I had a year of that schedule and when Jessica turned two I decided I was done. I did not want to miss one more day of her life.

I quit my job and went back on government assistance to focus on school. Jesse and I tried to give it another chance at living together. There were some apartments in front of my mom's house and he convinced me that I would be close to my mom but lived as a family with him. He went through the whole speech about how much he missed me and Jessica and how much he loved me. That confused me a little because people who loved each other would not hurt each other. But the part of me that grew up in a home where there was domestic violence everyday said that maybe it could work. I just did not know if and when that would happen.

I was afraid of him hurting me physically, but I was more afraid of the verbal abuse. I always hoped though that things would change. All I really had was hope. We moved to an apartment across from my mom's house. I figured living close to my mom's would be safe.

The apartment was nicer than the previous one, but much as I tried to make it cozy, it still didn't feel like it was my home, nor did I feel as comfortable as I did with my mom. I spent a lot of my time at my mom's since she continued babysitting Jessica. Jesse did not like me at my mom's so much so we fought about that. We also fought about chores and time he spent out. Things escalated one day and again violence prevailed. He dragged me across the apartment and kicked me on the thigh. He managed to drag me across to the door and pushed me out of the apartment. My hair was tousled and my clothes stretched out and torn. My face was covered with running makeup. I got up off the balcony floor and walked to my mom's house. She was not there so that gave me a chance to gather myself together and wash my face. Jessica was still in the apartment with Jesse. He had never hurt her and my gut feeling was that he wouldn't ever.

Since the day she was born she had been his pride and joy. He loved her completely. I felt safe to leave her there overnight. I explained to my mother that we had a fight and that I needed to spend the night at her house. She knew the severity of it, but she decided to let me make my own decisions on what to do next. The next morning, as I began to get dressed, I noticed that the entire front of my thigh was bruised. My whole thigh from top to bottom was black and blue. The weather was still hot during that time, but the only thing I could wear were pants. I had to hide the bruises. The days were horribly hot and wearing pants was not comfortable. Somehow, I managed to find some sweat pants and by that time, Jesse had brought Jessica over so my mother could babysit her.

I went to the apartment and gathered all my things and moved back in with my mom. She did not ask any questions. I did not want to answer any. Jesse moved out the following week because he could not afford to pay the rent. We did not speak for a while after that, and the only time I would see him would be when he would come to see Jessica. Even then it was from afar because he was not allowed beyond the gate. My stepfather had set that rule. It took nearly a month for the bruise to go away. For almost one month that summer I had to wear pants every day or sweat pants at night. A few friends saw my bruise and felt sorry for me. But nothing could compare to how sorry I felt for myself. Jessica was now two and I was starting another semester at ELAC.

I await another beginning.

ABOUT THE AUTHOR

Elva Alicia Leon is a living testament to the power of the spirit to overcome any obstacle. Growing up in gritty neighborhoods in East Los Angeles as a first-generation Mexican American, Leon and her two older sisters were raised in an abusive family environment plagued by alcoholism and violence. Leon was placed in a foster home at age nine, struggled with learning in school, was the victim of bullying, and attempted suicide at age fifteen. She became a teen parent at sixteen  and survived eight years of domestic abuse from the father of her child. Raising her daughter alone while attending school, she sometimes lived off on government assistance and continued to suffer from low self-esteem and extreme bouts of depression.

At age twenty-eight, the death of her fifteen-year-old stepson became a catalyst for change. Leon began a quest to understand death and life after death, which ultimately led to finding happiness and peace.

Leon has devoted her career to helping students with backgrounds similar to her own. An elementary school teacher in the community where she grew up, she has a BA in psychology from California State University, Los Angeles; a MA in education from Point Loma Nazarene University, San Diego; a Multiple Subject Teaching Credential; and a Pupil Personnel Services Credential that allows her to work as a career counselor. For fourteen years she taught first through sixth grades at Title I schools in Los Angeles, where the majority of the students are first-generation Mexican Americans.

Leon teaches arts, English language development, and physical education. She has been handling first grade for the last two years and before that sixth grade for four years. She also serves as motivational speaker, counselor, and grief counselor. She has mentored students who have suffered through everything from physical abuse to attempted suicide, cutting themselves, being involved in sexual relationships at an early age, and more. Although this is not part of her job description, Leon feels the need to be there as more than a teacher; she has an open-door policy that allows students to freely enter and discuss personal problems or concerns. She has worked with adults as well, teaching at El Monte/Rosemead adult school in the High School Diploma department. As a successful role model to her students, she provides inspiration and hope.

Her career also includes work for the state-funded Extended Opportunity Program & Services Department, which provides career counseling services to low-income students, and the Cooperative Agencies Resources for Education program, for low-income students who are also parents, in East Los Angeles.

Leon is the mother of a beautiful twenty-two-year-old daughter, Jessica, and lives in West Covina, California. She is Reiki Level 1 certified, fluent in Spanish, a member of Toastmasters. Leon loves to travel, meditates regularly, and continues to work on becoming the best version of herself.

If you or anyone you know is a victim of domestic violence, please get help.

Los Angeles County
Domestic Violence Hotline
800-978-3600

Project Sister
909-626-4357

Chicana Services 310-264-6644

If you are having thoughts of suicide, please get help.

National Suicide Prevention Lifeline
800-273-8255 or text Answer to 839863

If you need help with an unplanned pregnancy, you can call:

American Pregnancy Helpline
866-942-6466
http://www.thehelpline.com
free and confidential

Planned Parenthood Federation of America
800-230-PLAN

18648124R00100